HOW TO KNOW EVERYTHING

Elke Wiss is a practical philosopher and internationally best-selling author. She leads workshops in practical philosophy and the art of asking questions, teaching Socratic dialogue within organisations and offering individual philosophic consultations. Wiss is also a producer, writer and director of podcasts, theatre productions, numerous articles, short stories, monologues and narrative philosophical poetry. *How to Know Everything* is her first book.

WHAT READERS ARE SAYING

'A great book for anyone who wants to better understand themselves and others!'

'A ray of hope in a time of dispute and polarisation.'

'I found this book so valuable! A real enrichment for my daily life.'

'Everyone should read this. What fascinating conversations we would have then!'

'What a gem this book is!'

'Highly recommended for anyone who usually gets bogged down in discussions, quarrels, disagreements that lead to nothing.'

'Elke Wiss makes practical philosophy manageable for everyone. A must read!'

'Its powerful message urges us to connect more with each other and with ourselves.'

'A cheerful, unconventional book.'

'An inspiring, easy-to-read book, full of practical exercises to get yourself started right away. For me it's a must read!'

'A clear and practical book for brave thinkers who want to start having better, deeper conversations.'

'A disarming and urgent book in today's world!'

'Some books can actually change your worldview or your daily actions, and as far as I'm concerned this is one of them. I recommend it to everyone.'

'Read this book, it will enrich your life!'

HOW TO KNOW EVERYTHING

Ancient wisdom for modern life,
from Socrates to Sherlock Holmes

ELKE WISS

Translated by David Doherty

arrow books

1 3 5 7 9 10 8 6 4 2

Arrow Books
20 Vauxhall Bridge Road
London SW1V 2SA

Arrow Books is part of the Penguin Random House group
of companies whose addresses can be found at
global.penguinrandomhouse.com.

First published in the United Kingdom by Arrow Books in 2021
(First published as *Socrates Op Sneakers* in the Netherlands
by Ambo|Anthos in 2020)

This publication has been made possible with financial support
from the Dutch Foundation for Literature.

N ederlands
letterenfonds
dutch foundation
for literature

www.penguin.co.uk

ISBN 9781787467682

Typeset in 11.53/16.8 pt Minion Pro
by Integra Software Services Pvt. Ltd, Pondhicherry

Printed and bound in Great Britain by Clays Ltd, Elcograf S.p.A.

The authorised representative in the EEA is Penguin Random House Ireland,
Morrison Chambers, 32 Nassau Street, Dublin D02 YH68.

Contents

PART THREE

PART FOUR

PART FIVE

… to be patient toward all that is unsolved in your heart and to try to love the *questions themselves* like locked rooms and like books that are written in a very foreign tongue. Do not now seek the answers, which cannot be given you because you would not be able to live them. And the point is, to live everything. *Live* the questions now. Perhaps you will then gradually, without noticing it, live along some distant day into the answer.

Rainer Maria Rilke, *Letters to a Young Poet*[1]

Introduction

Out beyond ideas of wrongdoing and rightdoing, there is a field. I'll meet you there.

Rumi, Persian Sufi poet and mystic[1]

'**G**O ON, ASK your question,' Socrates said over my shoulder. 'Just do it. You've got every reason to.'

I blinked. 'Look, Socrates,' I explained, 'I know you're from about two thousand five hundred years ago, so maybe you've missed a trick or two, but these days that's not something you can just go ahead and ask …'

This was a good few years ago. I had signed up for a course in 'Practical Philosophy', my introduction to the concept. I was hoping to gain some theory and practical know-how about holding philosophical conversations and clarifying my thinking. As a writer and director of stage plays, I also wanted to get a clearer handle on my own thinking during the creative process of putting a performance together.

Perhaps, more to the point, I wanted to be more precise in the questions I asked my actors. So there I was, trying to get to grips with the practical side of philosophy.

On the first day of the course we broke for lunch and I found myself sharing a table with five classmates: four women and one man. Before long, the conversation turned to the topic of children. We went round the table. Do you have children? Yeah, one son. What about you? Two daughters, quite a handful! Everyone was asked a few follow-up questions: How old are they? Are they already at school? Does yours have an iPad yet?

It was the kind of chit-chat I knew well. I was in my late twenties and I'd already had a bunch of conversations just like it. As soon as someone says, 'No, I don't have kids', there's either an awkward silence or the Q&A quickly moves on to the next person. It never failed to surprise me: people with children love talking about having children, but it seems that we prefer to leave the stories of childless people untold. Even then I used to think: hang on a sec, everyone has a story to tell. What makes us decide on someone else's behalf, by not asking them a single question, that *their* story doesn't need to be heard?

Soon it was my turn and I duly said that I didn't have children. I took a breath, all set to say a bit more about myself. At the time I taught a lot of theatre classes in schools and I was brimming over with great stories about kids. Stories I was more than happy to share.

I was also eager to hear about other people's experiences and what motivated them in life. And to share my doubts about whether or not I should have children. I mean, how do you know if it's what you really want? It seems like such a big step. A defining moment. Something you really have to think about. How do you arrive at a decision like that?

But before I could open my mouth, the words 'And what about you?' had hastily been directed at the next participant. Everyone switched their focus to the woman next to me, who was soon chatting enthusiastically about her seven-year-old. Everyone studiously avoided catching my eye: apparently my story had no place in this conversation.

I found that strange. After all, we were more or less the same age and shared at least one interest, given that we had all signed up for the same course. Surely this was an ideal opportunity for more in-depth discussion, in a setting where you needn't be hemmed in by the standard tropes and habits of conversation.

A kind of indignation began bubbling up inside me. Why start a conversation about children and then only include a select few? Why would you tacitly determine whose stories are told and whose stories are passed over? Why not let each person decide for themselves whether or not they have something to share?

Once the woman beside me had said all she had to say about her little girl, the question was put to the next person – a woman in her early forties, with playful brown curls.

'No,' she said, 'I don't have kids,' and instantly the group was all set to move on.

That was when time stood still and I heard a voice behind me say, 'Go on, ask your question.' Socrates flashed me an encouraging smile. There was a twinkle of enjoyment in his eyes as he watched me squirm. 'Just do it! You've got every reason to.'

I looked at him and explained that was simply not the done thing in our day and age. 'I can't just come out with a question like that ...'

Socrates raised an eyebrow. 'That's the whole problem with you guys. You've come up with this code of conduct that labels some questions uncomfortable and inappropriate, while others are positive and permissible. And all because you think you have to spare people's feelings – that questions have to be polite. That you have to avoid subjects that are real and maybe even painful. When that's exactly what makes them so important.'

'Yes, but ...'

'The question you want to ask is factual, right?'

'Well ... yes ...'

'So how can a question of fact be inappropriate?'

'I ... uh ... I don't know.'

'Exactly. The question "Did you choose not to have children?" isn't all that different from "Did you choose not to celebrate your birthday? Or not to pursue your studies? Or not to take that promotion?" The fact that you've attached painful emotions to that particular subject, and made it an unwritten rule to tiptoe around it, has nothing to do with the question itself. No wonder you guys feel the need for more depth in your lives. You've turned conversation into a minefield! For fear of triggering an explosion, you keep everything as safe as can be. But when you do that, your conversations become superficial. And boring into the bargain.'

I opened my mouth to defend myself, but Socrates went right on without batting an eyelid. 'Besides, if you think people without children have as much right to tell their stories, but you keep your mouth shut, that makes you part of the problem. You're just as guilty of keeping that unwritten rule alive.'

I blinked again, a little dazed. Now what?

'Ask the question,' Socrates sighed, nodding at the woman with the playful curls and leaning back in his chair.

Oblivious to the art of asking questions, but with a dose of good intentions and a desire to grow as a person, I decided, encouraged by Socrates, to give it a try. The revolution starts here, I thought. I'll take a stand for childless women in group discussions everywhere. Not to mention adding some depth to this particular discussion. I summoned up my courage, took a deep breath, looked Playful Curls straight in the eye and broke the momentary silence in the group. 'And was it your own choice not to have children?'

Another silence followed, tense and awkward this time. I could feel the rest of the group holding their breath. The woman glared at me, seemed to freeze, then said between clenched teeth, 'No. It wasn't my own choice, no.'

The others made a collective effort to turn invisible. No small feat for six people crowded round a small table, but they gave it their best shot.

I felt my own nerves spiralling out of control. 'Great advice, pal!' I hissed at Socrates. 'Thanks for nothing.' Alarm bells started going off in my head. How on earth was I going to salvage this situation?

Lunch was well and truly over, and we headed back to class as a group. I made a point of falling into step with Playful Curls and stammered something along the lines of 'I didn't mean to hurt your feelings. I just feel that in discussions like this people who don't have kids are so often passed over and I really don't think that's fair, and I always want to know more about people's stories and, because I was genuinely interested in your experiences, I thought I'd just go ahead and ask ... because, well, everyone deserves to be heard and we're here to learn about practical philosophy after all and to ask better questions and ...'

Stumbling through a minefield of my own making, I don't think I managed to formulate one coherent thought. My cowardly, shame-faced apology remained hovering somewhere in mid-air. She gave a curt nod, a sign that I could stop talking, then added in a fierce whisper, 'You know, I think it's very strange that people assume they have the right to ask a question like that.' She strode off towards the classroom and left me to straggle along behind her.

That lunchtime encounter, that conversation and that question have stayed with me so clearly because they stirred such powerful feelings – in the woman I was talking to, and in me.

I felt ashamed, I felt guilty, though it was hard to say exactly why. My intentions had been pure: I had wanted to connect and create a more open, more meaningful conversation. To share our stories. To go beyond the superficial chit-chat of 'What do you do for a living?', 'Where do you live?' and 'How many kids do you have?' I had wanted to make room for everyone's stories. To question an unwritten rule that had begun to seem unfair to me. Like a modern-day Socrates, I had wanted to conquer the world with good questions, worthwhile answers and better conversation.

During that fateful lunch break I wish I had known what I know now. That there *is* a way to ask that kind of question without dragging the other person through a swamp of unwelcome emotions. That it *is* possible to create a context and conditions in which you can move beyond small talk and strike a deeper chord. That you *can* ask questions that connect, questions that allow you to say what's really on your mind, even if it hurts a little sometimes. That you *can* look at questions differently, and find ways of asking them that are less likely to prompt a defensive response. That *good* questions lead to strong answers that deserve your fullest attention. That there *is* a way to have a conversation on equal terms, one in which essential ideas and beliefs are held up to the light. A way to get to the heart of the matter, to distinguish sense from nonsense – an approach that allows everyone to take responsibility for their own emotions and sensitivities. A way to let the question simply be what it is: an invitation to dig a little deeper.

It's an invitation you are free to turn down or accept. Without the need for painful silences, wounded souls or praying to turn yourself invisible at a lunch table so small that there's no room to hide.

If I had known then what I know now, I would still have asked that question. But I'd have asked it differently. As Socrates often did, I would have asked permission. I would have said, 'I'd be interested to hear more. Do you mind if I ask you about it?'

But I didn't know then what I know now. I did the best I could with the tools to hand and the result was a painful experience, one I have often thought long and hard about since. In the years that followed, that brief exchange made a huge contribution to my personal development, my education and even this book. Since then I have gone on to learn more about practical philosophy, the art of asking questions and of holding philosophical and Socratic conversations. I studied in the Netherlands and abroad. I founded a company called De Denksmederij (The Thinksmiths) and gave training courses and workshops in Socratic discourse, critical thinking and asking questions. Every day since then has been part of a learning process. Learning what works and what doesn't. What constitutes a good question. What you can do to bring depth to a discussion and get people thinking, philosophising together and connecting with one another. And I got to know Socrates, who is something of a hero to me now. He is my Beyoncé of philosophy, and I am most definitely a fan.

During training sessions, philosophical consultations and presentations, I have seen and felt for myself the impact of holding a conversation with a different intention, and how conversations can change for the better when you actively cultivate a Socratic attitude and work on your approach to asking questions. I have seen and felt how much more substantial and meaningful conversations can be when you become aware of the all-too-human pitfalls around listening and having a conversation, and discover how to avoid them.

I experienced the joy of sharing that knowledge with other people, and equipping them with those insights and skills. As time went on, I realised I wanted to write a book to help everyone who longs to have better conversations but doesn't yet quite know how to make them happen. Let me take you on that journey. With Socrates as our guide, we will explore the art of asking questions. So that in any situation, under any circumstances, you will know how to bring depth to a conversation, and how to understand a bit more about the world around you – to know everything a little more deeply – by asking what needs to be asked.

PRACTICAL PHILOSOPHY: WHAT USE IS THAT?

Practical philosophy is not some esoteric school of thought reserved for bearded old guys in ivory towers. Practical philosophy embraces important ideas like justice, friendship, inclusivity and courage and links them to questions that we find ourselves asking in practical everyday life. Is it okay to lie to a friend? Does my company need a more inclusive hiring policy? When is it best to keep something to yourself? Is this the right time to change jobs? Does the way I behave really reflect who I am? Should I be putting my own interests first in this situation?

We've all been there. At a crossroads where our own personal dilemmas and life's big questions intersect. Every one of these questions is central to our lives, but good luck in googling the answers! These sorts of questions can quickly make you think yourself into a corner.

Enter practical philosophy. It's my belief that the best way to look for these kinds of answers is by talking things through with someone who asks the right questions, so that you can become wiser together. I want to share with you a particular way of having conversations, of joining together with others in a search for wisdom, new insights and answers to essential questions.

But this is not a book that will help you dazzle people with small talk. What it *will* do is help you tap into the hidden depths in your conversations. When you explore new possibilities and perspectives, when your own thinking is 'switched on', the deeper layers of a conversation open up and you start to see the potential for new discoveries and surprising insights. It's a kind of flexible thinking where you decide to switch your point of view or jump aboard another person's train of thought to see where it takes you, and have a discussion without the desire to convince the other person or to come out on top.

Writer Lammert Kamphuis gets to the heart of practical philosophy: 'Spanish philosopher José Ortega y Gasset once said that philosophy is the science of the superficial: when you philosophise, you bring unconscious ideas, assumptions and beliefs to the surface.'[2]

It is both worthwhile and rewarding not only to become aware of your own unconscious ideas about human nature, but also to leave space for other people's ideas, too. It's a skill I like to call 'agile perspective': the ability to think outside your own framework, opinions and views. And philosophising is the perfect way to train it. Agile perspective is all about exploring and investigating the other person's point of view, without immediately becoming caught up in your own opinions. It's about letting go of your personal feelings for a moment, and exploring an issue clearly and calmly, keeping your slate as blank as possible. And when your own opinions do arise, it's about questioning them critically and discovering that you have a much broader mind than you thought.

In other words, this is a book for brave thinkers. For people who dare to doubt, and who are eager to investigate something instead of assuming they know it for sure already. Who are happy to embrace not-knowing something. For people who have the courage not to pipe up right away, but to keep quiet for a while and listen. Who then take that quiet moment as the starting point for a question that digs a little deeper, that shows they want to know more. In the knowledge that philosophising – not-knowing, asking questions, searching for answers – makes you a richer, wiser person. It's a book for everyone who isn't content to insist, 'This is my truth', but who wants to go in search of shared wisdom.

Albert Einstein once said, 'If I had an hour to solve a problem and my life depended on the solution, I would spend the first fifty-five minutes determining the proper question to ask.' This book will help you ask questions that matter. Important questions. Questions that invite, explore, unravel, reveal, confront, deepen, challenge, excite and set things in motion. This book will train you to think, analyse and

question critically. It will provide you with practical guide-
lines, conditions, techniques, theoretical backgrounds and
ways of listening. And it will serve as a compass to point
you towards further exploration and philosophical depth in
your day-to-day discussions.

What it won't do is supply you with a simple checklist of
questions guaranteed to hit the bull's-eye. There are none.
A question that is bang on target in one situation can completely miss the mark in another. Believe me, I know.

WHY SOCRATES?

Welcome to your practical manual for developing an enquiring attitude and asking better questions. With the philosopher
Socrates as your guide and teacher. Picture him in sneakers,
stilettos, cowboy boots … whatever floats your boat.

Socrates, the Ancient Greek thinker who lived some 2,500
years ago. One of the world's most practical philosophers,
who haunted the squares and markets of Athens trying
to engage people in philosophical discussions, to seize the
moment and get to grips with what really matters in life.
He was quick to acknowledge his own lack of expertise and
adopted an enquiring attitude with the sole aim of questioning others about their knowledge and wisdom. Socrates
asked questions – lots of questions. He understood the art
of asking questions like no other. He had two main reasons
for taking this approach:

1. He wanted to be wiser. Operating on the principle 'I know that I do not know anything', Socrates went in search of true knowledge. He realised that true knowledge arises from dialogue and saw his partner in conversation as first and foremost the whetstone on which to sharpen his own thinking.

2. He wanted to free his conversation partner from the errors in their reasoning, their flawed thinking and their attempts to kid themselves and others (i.e. their bullshit). He helped them go in search of 'true knowledge'. Through his critical questioning, they came to understand that what they thought they knew for certain was not true knowledge at all.

In our modern world, where we all think we know the score, and where opinions receive more airtime than facts, we could definitely do with a healthy dose of openness, curiosity and not-knowingness. Socrates and his practical approach to philosophising, thinking and asking questions provide the perfect touchstone. From him we can learn how to develop an enquiring attitude that's full of wonder, and find ways to ask critical questions of each other and of ourselves.

Socrates: a most practical philosophy

Socrates, our hero, lived in Athens around 2,500 years ago. He was born in the year 469 BCE. His father was a sculptor, his mother a midwife. He grew up, married a woman called Xanthippe and together they had three sons. Initially Socrates followed in his father's footsteps and became a craftsman, but he soon turned to the art of instruction. In the *agora*, the heart of political and cultural life in the city, he entered into conversation with anyone who would listen – administrators, merchants, politicians, craftsmen, artists and students – to discuss fundamental aspects of their lives and work. By asking questions, Socrates gave people the opportunity to account for their decisions, to reflect on the justifications for their behaviour and to set out the reasoning that led to their points of view. This brought him much respect, but not everyone was a big fan of his probing way of asking questions. It earned him the nickname 'the gadfly of Athens'.

Socrates believed that the only thing that makes us truly happy is knowing what is right; our inner ability to distinguish the good in every situation. Human beings want to be good at what they do. How do you become a good father or a good friend? How do you know what choice to make as a manager or business owner? What does right and responsible action mean to you, as a doctor? Socrates was a master of questioning and embodying a questioning attitude. If there were an all-time championship of not-knowing, he would win hands down. He had an unrivalled ability to hold up a mirror to whomever he was talking and reflect their own words and contradictions back at them. He didn't bang on about what he knew, but kept on asking questions, inviting his partner in conversation to enter into a joint enquiry.

Socrates's motto was 'I know that I know nothing' and it earned him the title of the wisest man of all, from the Oracle of Delphi. The Oracle was located at the centre of Delphi, a site of sacred worship for the Ancient Greeks. It was a highly venerated oracle, dedicated to Apollo, who was the god of prophecy and oracles, among many other things. Thousands of people, many of them pilgrims, flocked to Delphi each year to consult the oracle and ask the gods for sound advice if they had important and difficult decisions to make. As he was also the god of the sun and of light itself, Apollo was thought to illuminate even the darkest corners and see those things that escape the gaze of mere mortals.

Socrates was thirsty for knowledge and wanted the answers to big questions such as 'What is justice?' His approach was to find someone who supposedly knew what they were talking about and get them to answer his question. A judge, for example, a person who passed judgement on matters of good and evil on a daily basis. Surely they would have an answer to the question of what justice is? The judge Socrates consulted did indeed have an answer for him and presented it in detail. But it wasn't long before Socrates began to point out contradictions in the judge's explanation. After a while, even the judge had to admit they no longer knew exactly how to describe the concept of justice. Was it a virtue? Did it have something to do with temperance? Had they themselves acted justly in this or that particular case? The list of doubts was endless. This was how Socrates got his interlocutors thinking, by engaging them in a collective search for wisdom.

Socrates therefore took a very practical approach to philosophising: he discussed abstract concepts by applying them to concrete situations. In his view, philosophy was not something reserved for the elite, but instead something that had to be useful and prove its worth in relation to practical everyday experiences. His aim was to hold a joint enquiry, working with others to weigh up arguments and engaging in a shared learning process and search for wisdom. The focus was always on concrete experience. Purely theoretical exchanges about ideas, concepts and hypothetical situations were pointless as far as Socrates was concerned. They did not produce true knowledge, but a kind of 'fake knowledge', restricted to traditional academia. In fact Socrates was carrying out behavioural analyses and, by questioning how people behaved and thought, he tried to distil the rules by which they were governed. And when you make these unconscious rules, beliefs, convictions and opinions explicit, when you question them and understand them better, this can also result in better behaviour.

Socrates argued that knowledge is not something you gain by parroting the ideas of others, but is instead more like an act of memory. That's why, although many of his dialogues were recorded by his student and protégé, the philosopher

Plato, there are in fact no books written by Socrates himself. He believed that writing books would only result in a rigid, academic and impractical kind of learning. The only way to attain true knowledge, in his view, was through dialogue. Knowledge was possessed by the immortal soul, and Socrates believed he was helping his conversation partners to recall that knowledge. His method came to be known by the wonderful word 'maieutics', from the Greek for 'to act as a midwife'.

Socrates's mother had been a midwife and so he was familiar with the process of childbirth and he often compared his work – drawing knowledge out of the other person – with delivering a child.

In *Meno*, Plato's account of a Socratic dialogue, Socrates says:

> Some things I have said of which I am not altogether confident. But that we shall be better and braver and less helpless if we think that we ought to enquire, than we should have been if we indulged in the idle fancy that there was no knowing and no use in searching after what we do not know; that is a theme upon which I am ready to fight, in word and deed, to the utmost of my power.[3]

Ultimately, it was a fight that cost Socrates his life. At the age of seventy he stood accused of godlessness and corrupting the youth of Athens. He was condemned for his practices and sentenced to death. Over the years he had antagonised many people with his critical questions. Some disparaged him as a sophist, a spreader of dubious arguments and wicked fallacies that encouraged the younger generation to defy authority. In their eyes, his conduct undermined the sacred laws of Athens. Yet more accusations decried Socrates for being undemocratic. For instance, he had once said that the procedure of arbitrarily selecting governors from among the people was no guarantee of a just outcome. On the whole, Socrates didn't exactly make many friends with his views and his way of speaking.

Plato's *Apology* gives an extensive account of the trial of Socrates. The philosopher pleaded his own case before a jury of 500 Athenian men. In his defence, Socrates explains how he came to have such a bad reputation and, in passing, has a dig at his prosecutors. He appears not to take the matter of his trial entirely seriously, and a majority of 360 condemn him to drink from the poison cup. Socrates was not afraid of death, reasoning that death is one of two things: either it is a kind of nothingness, a dreamless eternal sleep, or the soul moves to a place where all the deceased are gathered. He argued that nothingness was not to be feared and nor was the alternative. The death of Socrates is regarded by some as philosophy's 'big bang' moment, thought of by many as the starting point for the history of philosophy.[4]

Plato recorded dozens of Socratic dialogues in writing. Of course we can never be entirely sure to what extent those exchanges actually took place and how much should be attributed to Plato's imagination. What we do know is that these accounts of how Socrates conducted his conversations have led to a structured method that we call 'Socratic dialogue'.

The German philosopher, educator and political activist Leonard Nelson (1882–1927) was the founder of the modern-day Socratic dialogue. His goal was to restore the Socratic method to its rightful place: not only as an abstract and theoretical entity within the history of philosophy, but also as a practical tool, a method that could be applied in education, organisations, politics and other areas of everyday life. He recognised that a Socratic enquiring attitude is what you need to develop in order to bring more wonder, reflection and depth to your conversations.

WHY BOTHER?

But why on earth would you want to train yourself to ask good questions and develop a philosophical attitude? We lead busy enough lives as it is, you might say. Even so, there are plenty of good reasons.

First of all, it's what the world needs now. This rapid-fire society of ours, with its tendency towards polarisation, can benefit hugely from slowing down, from a fundamentally philosophical attitude, from people who are genuinely interested in each other and who know how to ask the right questions. The public debate, talk shows, interviews, opinion pieces, online and offline discussions and even our heated conversations over dinner: all too often they take the form of attack and defence, amounting to little more than mud-slinging fuelled by a ragbag of opinions or a tug-of-war between opposing views. None of this is especially productive, connective or helpful. When the dust has settled, everyone retreats to their own corner to cool off and sinks even deeper into their own closed views rather than opening up to the other person's experience.

So many of us are ready and willing to have a good conversation about the themes of the day: about racism and the aftermath of colonialism, about discrimination, gender, body shaming, #MeToo, refugees and migrants or the climate crisis. These are the sorts of topics that seem to inflame tempers all too quickly, push people's buttons and make them determined to be understood, instead of first trying to understand the other person's point of view. For our own sake and the sake of the world we live in, we need to find better ways to have these conversations. We need to pay more attention, listen more closely and try to understand *before* we are understood.

We need to ask good questions that lead to deeper understanding. Without them, we wind up losing touch with our creativity, our powers of imagination and our ability to think critically.

Asking focused questions helps us develop these skills and conduct richer, freer and more complex conversations in ways that are more effective and more nuanced. This book is designed to help you grow in these areas.

Femke Halsema has been a leading light of Dutch politics for many years. Having bowed out of the parliamentary arena a few years ago, she returned to public life in 2018 as Mayor of Amsterdam. In an interview in 2019 with the current-affairs weekly *Vrij Nederland*, she talked about a debate she had recently had with the rising star of the populist right, Thierry Baudet:

> I really immerse myself in other people's point of view. I ran into Thierry Baudet last year, a few weeks after our debate in Amsterdam, and he told me 'You came out of that debate much better than I did.' I thought that was very noble of him. 'Do you know why?' I asked. 'There's a big difference between you and me. I take a genuine interest in you and your views, so I prepared thoroughly. But you have absolutely no interest in me.' He sees me as a symbol of something he hates, without knowing what I actually stand for.[5]

Femke Halsema's attitude is one we seldom see, whereas the attitude she attributes to her opponent, Baudet, is one we see all too often. We know too little about each other and although we are barely even interested in the other person's opinion, we have already decided we don't like it at all. Without actually knowing why.

The attitude of curiosity, of wanting to ask questions, of wanting to explore the other person's point of view, begins right here with us. With you and me. In our conversations with friends, family, at the dinner table, at work or down the pub. And from there, this new Socratic style of talking, of wanting to become wiser together, will hopefully ease its way into debates, talk shows, newspaper columns and the political arena. This change for the better can start with us.

A second reason to develop these skills is simple: the quality of your conversations will improve enormously! When you and the family sit down at the dinner table together, wouldn't it be nice to have a more interesting conversation once in a while than 'How was school today?' or 'Busy day at work?' Conversations in pubs, in classrooms, in the media and at birthday parties become much more enjoyable if you develop your curiosity and start to ask a different kind of question. Mastering a more thoughtful approach to questions gives you a passport to the other person's world of experience. You can genuinely get to know each other, discover new things and arrive at surprising insights and exciting new ways of thinking. Sharing this with each other makes you a richer human being.

The third reason? It's fun! Thinking and asking, practising practical philosophy, is honest-to-goodness fun. One of my students even called it addictive. It's the feeling that your thinking is becoming clearer and clearer, that you can get to the heart of the matter more effectively and separate sense from nonsense. The feeling that you are gaining new insights, developing ideas and finding new ways to investigate issues and arrive at solutions together with other people. All this is enriching, interesting and thoroughly enjoyable. You create space to think; room to be more flexible, agile and light on your feet.

Discovering and exploring someone else's thought processes, taking someone else on a joint quest for wisdom, is a game like no other. There is an intrinsic value to the act of practical philosophising, the infinite questioning of situations, claims and statements. It's a bit like playing the piano. Why do you play the piano? Because it's a great thing to do. Why engage in practical philosophy? Because it's a great thing to do. Probing an issue by asking questions is not unlike solving a sudoku puzzle: the more you do it, the better you get, and the process is as rewarding as the result.

And then there's the fourth and final reason: by asking good questions and following through in a collective, conversational search for wisdom, you get to know yourself better. Looking at the world with a sense of wonder, and questioning everything critically, doesn't provide you with ready-made answers, but it does give you the tools to explore ideas and discover the answers for yourself.

I believe that good questions create a real and genuine connection. A connection that recognises our differences and our similarities, that gets to the essence of who we are. In the words of Brené Brown, researcher of shame, courage, vulnerability, love and, in short, everything that makes us human: we are hard-wired for connection. Above all else, we want to feel meaningfully connected to our fellow human beings. And if this world of ours needs anything at present, surely that is it.

This book is here to help. In the first part I look at why, usually, we are so bad at asking good questions. What is it that makes us avoid asking questions altogether? How can the simple act of asking a question be so difficult, awkward or downright terrifying?

Over the next four parts we'll roll up our sleeves and get stuck in. In Part Two you'll work on the core of this approach, the jumping-off point for asking good questions and philosophising: developing a Socratic questioning attitude.

Part Three will equip you with a range of highly useful skills that set the basic conditions for asking good, in-depth questions that start things in motion. You will train yourself to listen, purely and simply. You will consider the importance of language as well as what we can learn from Sherlock Holmes when it comes to pursuing an incisive line of enquiry.

The fourth part centres on technical tips and tricks. There you will learn the techniques associated with asking clear, complete and in-depth questions, how to use 'echo questions' and why they work so well, and how to recognise and steer clear of questioning pitfalls.

Finally, in Part Five we look at the next step: you've asked a good question, now what? It's time for conversation. And there's much to be said about that, too. How do you keep your conversation interesting? How do you enter into a practical philosophical enquiry that leaves both of you that little bit wiser?

PART ONE

Why are we so bad at asking good questions?

Is there not here conceit of knowledge, which is a disgraceful sort of ignorance?

Socrates[1]

So what exactly is our problem? Are we really that bad at asking good questions? If so, how come? And, more importantly, is there any hope for us?

In this section we ask: What is a question anyway? Why do we avoid asking questions? And when we *do* ask questions, why are they often not all that good?

'I ask questions all day long. What could I possibly learn?'

I love my work. When I'm at a party or a networking event and someone asks me what I do for a living, I inevitably launch into an enthusiastic spiel: 'I help people ask better questions. By taking a philosophical approach. I give work-shops, courses, personal coaching to help people understand their thought processes and—' Often that's when the other person interrupts. 'You *help* people ask questions? But what's the big deal? I ask questions all day long. Why would I need to take a course in that?'

A little part of me wants to play the smart alec and point out the irony: for someone who insists they need no help asking questions, they have just produced a string of questions that are leading, rhetorical and anything but open and curious. Questions that barely qualify as genuine questions, really. Instead I try to see encounters like this as a reminder of how much work is left to do, and how much more we all could learn, when it comes to asking really good questions.

Our friend at the party is right, of course. We do ask questions all day long. At least we *think* we do.

Even if you're convinced that you are someone who asks questions all day long and are bound to be good at it, the truth is likely to be very disappointing. More often than not, what you are really doing is delivering a sentence with a question mark tacked on the end. And no one needs a course to do that. Breathing is something else we do all the time, yet study after study has shown that we are not especially good at it: most of our breathing is too rapid and too shallow. It's a similar story when we ask questions. Our unconscious habits lead us astray.

Asking questions is not a skill that we, as a society, have mastered very well at all. We ask too many questions out of the blue, and often they are incomplete, suggestive, rhetorical, ill-timed or questions that aren't questions at all. 'Don't you think Tom's been irritable lately?' 'Why would I do it any other way?' 'What's your excuse this time?' 'Don't you think Mike's put on weight?' 'Do you think Anna didn't come because she's scared? Or is it that she's angry, or maybe she's …?'

When someone presents us with a problem or a dilemma, instead of asking them what's wrong, we often fly into fixer mode. 'Have you tried talking to her?' 'That therapist helped me a lot, I'm sure they could help you too!' Or we swamp the other person with advice. 'You know what you should do? You should …' 'You're just going to have to call such-and-such.' Or we overlay the other person's story with our own experiences. 'The exact same happened to me! Only in my case it was more …'

We'd much rather convince the other person that we know what we're talking about than take a closer look at their own point of view. We hear their story and immediately establish a link to our own lives, instead of sticking with what they are trying to tell us. Our mind is already skipping ahead, thinking about what we're going to say as soon as they stop talking:

'Yes, but I have a completely different take on these things …!' When instead we could simply take the time to really listen.

The good news is: asking the right questions is something you can learn. The ability to ask questions may be innate, but it's also a skill that rewards practice. It's kind of like doing the high jump: in theory it's something almost every human being can have a bash at from an early age. But we'd be so much better at it if we'd thought about how to approach it and trained our natural ability.

Questions are like tools. The right ones can allow you to get into a thoughtful discussion and explore another person's point of view. You could opt for a delicate set of tweezers or a cheeky drill bit, be as subtle as sandpaper or as confrontational as a crowbar. As with any tool, the result will depend on how you use it. I can take up a chisel and chip away at a lump of stone to create a sculptural work of art, but if I get carried away and apply too much force in the wrong way, I might accidentally knock my statue's head off. Alternatively, I can take my sandpaper and rub away at a surface all I like, but if I don't apply enough pressure, nothing much will really change. It's the same with questions: they are all the more effective when handled with skill and a sense of purpose.

A question that arises out of genuine curiosity is a step in the other person's direction. By asking that kind of question, you are actually saying: I want to come closer and get to know you better. That inevitably involves risk and creates a little tension. After all, the other person could easily tell you to get lost. And that's one of the main reasons why we are so hesitant to ask good questions.

What exactly is a question?

It's worth taking a moment to think about what a question is and, more importantly, what it's not. It's easy to assume that we know what we mean by the word 'question', but on closer inspection, many of the questions we ask are not really questions at all. Instead they are often statements, assumptions or hypotheses in disguise. 'Don't you think Alice is right?' 'Are you implying that …?' 'Ben does have a point, doesn't he?' These are more like opinions packaged as questions, or hypotheses in need of a quick check. When you see them in black and white, this might speak for itself. 'Duh, of course those aren't real questions! Anyone can see that!' But listen closely from now on and you'll start to hear how many of these questions we ask on a daily basis, as opposed to questions that are genuine questions.

The *Oxford English Dictionary* defines 'question' as 'a sentence worded or expressed so as to elicit information from a person'. While this is a perfectly acceptable account of what a question is – I'm not about to mess with the *OED*! – it stops short of talking about how that sentence might be handled, the intention behind it or the effect on the other person. In the context of practical philosophy and our focus, here, on how to ask good questions, I have come up with the following definition:

- A question is an invitation. An invitation to think, explain, sharpen, dig deeper, provide information, investigate, connect.
- A good question is clearly formulated and is born of an open, curious attitude.
- A good question remains focused on the other person and their story.
- A good question gets someone thinking.
- A good question leads to clarification, new insights or a new perspective for the recipient.
- A good question is *not* intended to give advice, check hypotheses, impose a point of view, share an opinion, make a suggestion or leave the other person feeling judged or cornered.

The last point is a particularly important one. This distinction may seem obvious, yet so many of the questions we ask on a daily basis fall into this exclusion zone. All too often, without meaning to or even realising we're doing it, we ask questions that centre on ourselves. On our own fears, feelings, ideas, prejudices, needs. Unknowingly, we use our questions to project these preoccupations onto the other person's story. In other words, we ask questions to reassure ourselves, instead of taking a closer look at or enquiring after what the other person is actually saying.

It's like your best friend listening to your account of a blazing row with your partner and coming back with: 'So you're thinking of leaving him?' Or the colleague who responds to your tale of a holiday in Tuscany with 'Weren't you sick of the sight of pasta and pizza after a week?' Or the friend who listens to your worries about your mother's failing health and says, 'So you're thinking of being her carer? That's tough, you know. I did it myself for a while ...'

No such thing as a bad question?

You often hear people say there's no such thing as a bad question and, on the whole, there's not a lot wrong with that statement. Usually it can be an invitation to fire away and not hold back, and of course that's a good thing. Questions aren't meant to be swallowed. However, many a well-meaning question is poorly phrased. Even when the intention behind the question is sound and the questioner's motives are impeccable, the question itself can miss the mark completely. As Oscar Wilde once wrote, 'There is no such thing as a moral or an immoral book. Books are well written or badly written.'[2] It's the same with questions. Questions are not inherently good or bad. But they can certainly be well or poorly formulated and put to good or bad use.

*

When I talk about 'good questions' in this book, I always mean genuine, sincere questions that encourage the other person to think. These are questions asked without the aim of influencing or steering things in a particular direction. There's no intention to fix a problem or impose your own way of thinking. A good question is one that is clearly recognisable as such, that works in the context in which it is asked and with an intention that is fit for purpose.

To give a list of concrete examples here would miss the point: a question that works extremely well in one context may not work at all well in another. What's appropriate in one situation is not always appropriate in another. The intention that comes through in one conversation as opposed to another also determines a question's effectiveness. Time and again, I come back to my own definition: *A question is an invitation.*

What constitutes an in-depth conversation?

In this book I will also talk to you about in-depth conversations: conversations with real substance, that get to the heart of a matter. It's worth taking a moment to think about what a good, in-depth conversation entails. A good conversation isn't boring or one-sided. It doesn't simply consist of two people juxtaposing opinions, swapping anecdotes, exchanging small talk, overlapping monologues or nattering away at the same time.

What an in-depth conversation *does* entail is an exploration of the experience of one of the participants and a closer examination of the ideas, concepts and questions at play, not least notions about human nature. Focusing on the other person's experience is actually trickier than it sounds as, without deliberately doing so, we might be too enthusiastic in sharing our own story, experience or viewpoint at the expense of exploring the other person's deep enough first. An in-depth conversation should be a stimulating and shared undertaking, and a joint search for wisdom.

However well-meaning, my dear old gran's response to the news that I sprained my ankle doesn't make the grade. 'Aw, pet, how awful for you. Greta's niece did the same thing last year. Out of commission for the best part of three weeks. Couldn't drive, couldn't walk – an invalid she was. Awful! Just awful!'

Why don't good questions come easily?

To get better at asking good questions it's important to understand why we're often not very good at it in the first place. If I want to be a star debater, I'd better resign myself to a lot of practice. But practice alone won't get me there. I also have to learn about the pitfalls, and get to grips with the theory by understanding how to conduct a debate and build a strong argument. To become a better cook, I have to supplement my practice in the kitchen with an understanding of how flavours, smells, textures and ingredients work together, and delve into the reasoning behind using particular combinations, tools and techniques. Anyone who has watched their attempt at a chocolate soufflé collapse before their very eyes will understand why concerning yourself with pitfalls and possible causes of failure is sometimes the best place to start.

So before we start practising the 'how' of asking good questions, it's worth stopping to reflect on why good questions don't come easily. Once you understand the reasons why so many often fall short in this department, you may realise that you also make many of these classic question missteps. That knowledge alone will make you more aware of your own abilities as a questioner and will help you sidestep the pitfalls. Not only that, but you'll soon be able to tune in more closely to the day-to-day conversations around you, as well as those in the media, and pick up a wealth of dos and don'ts when it comes to asking good questions.

When writing this book, I appealed for feedback, conducted interviews and asked all kinds of questions. Two of the most important were 'What stops you asking a question?' and 'Why do you think people hold back on asking questions?' Combining the responses I received with my own research, experience, discoveries and conclusions, I came up with six reasons why we are sometimes incapable of asking good questions:

1. **HUMAN NATURE:** Talking about yourself feels so much nicer than asking questions.
2. **FEAR OF ASKING:** Posing a question can be a scary proposition.
3. **SCORING POINTS:** An opinion makes more of an impression than a question.
4. **LACK OF OBJECTIVITY:** Our ability to reason objectively is in decline.
5. **IMPATIENCE:** We think asking good questions is a waste of time.
6. **LACK OF COMPETENCE:** Nobody teaches us how.

REASON ONE: HUMAN NATURE

We're just too selfish to ask good questions

Not the most positive note to start on, but it's true: we are often too self-centred to ask good questions. Asking a good question means a willingness to step into another person's world and explore their thoughts and experiences. And, as a rule, we simply don't find their world as interesting as our own. We are concerned with our own opinions, our own perceptions, our own identity, our own story. There are several conversational giveaways that reveal our reluctance to ask and our habit of focusing on ourselves.

Interrupting, rattling on, repeating your own point of view

Some people are champions at it: inviting you to talk, only to interrupt within seconds and rattle on about themselves.

'How was your trip to the islands? Do anything nice?'

'Yeah, we went to this great music festival. And there was a lovely bike path that ran along the coast and—'

'Oh, Jake and I went up there for that same festival years ago. It must have been one of the first trips we took together. Loved it. But it was so cold at night! Freezing in fact! We hadn't thought to bring our warm coats. I mean it was June, for goodness' sake, how cold could it be? Well, we learned the hard way how the weather can turn up there ...'

We all know what a great way this is to kill a conversation stone-dead. I've yet to meet the person who says, 'They're such great company. I just love the way they interrupt me as soon as I start talking. And the way they rattle on and on, and keep repeating their own point of view ... I mean, how great is that! I just love them!'

Yet as obviously irritating as this behaviour is, we seldom stop to dwell on where it comes from. It's a symptom of not listening. As soon as you interrupt, you've abandoned any attempt to understand the other person and are only interested in speaking yourself. And by rattling on, you take over the conversation completely and leave the other person no room to engage in a dialogue. By repeating your own point of view over and over again, all you are proving is how little you care about the other person's perspective.

Thinking about what you're going to say while the other person is still talking

Sometimes you're already thinking about what you are going to say before the other person has finished speaking. 'I want to pick up on that point they made to start with, because I really don't agree and I have a few points of my own to make on that score and I must get them in, because otherwise I'll forget what I wanted to say and it's about bloody time someone understood where I stand on this issue.'

This is another sign that you have zoned out and are only half-listening at best. You're busy thinking about yourself, not engaging with the other person. And you're not alone! Often we only hear the first two sentences spoken by another person before our thoughts start racing and our brain goes in search of our own opinions, anecdotes and ideas.

ANNA: I quit my job today. It was really nerve-racking but I was kind of proud of myself for being so brave. I built up my courage for days and finally marched into my supervisor's office and told her.

WALTER: Do you have anything lined up?

ANNA: No, not yet. But …

WALTER: If you ask me, that wasn't a very smart move. I mean, why throw away what you have when there's nothing on the horizon. I just don't think it's wise, especially now, when everything's so uncertain.

ANNA: It's not that bad. I weighed up the pros and cons before I made my decision. And I took some time to think about what really matters to me.

Let's face it, there's no real dialogue going on here. In the end, many a conversation amounts to little more than switching back and forth between two monologues. And no, two monologues don't add up to a dialogue.

The help-and-advice reflex

When confronted with someone else's problem in the course of a conversation, many people react like a bull to a red rag: they charge at it head-on. Not with questions that might help illuminate the situation, but with guidance, help and advice.

'You know what you should do? Get on the phone to such-and-such. And have you tried …?'

The intention is noble enough, but it does testify to a certain degree of egocentricity: the responder is primarily concerned with 'solving' and 'fixing' when they could be listening, trying to get to grips with the problem and asking questions about the mindset, motives and experiences of the person they are talking to. In the end, the advice given usually says everything about the person giving it and very little about the person sharing their problem or predicament. Although our intentions are often to offer help or advice, the other person may not be asking for or interested in our so-called 'help'.

Later on, in Part Two, I talk more about why our impulse to give out advice in these situations doesn't always work out the way we'd intended it to. There we look at the different kinds of empathy in greater depth and discover why sometimes it might not always be the best solution or response, even though we think it is.

Psychologist Huub Buijssen, who has written a whole book on the subject,[3] has this to say on the matter:

> We often can't wait to give someone advice. We seem to think that's what the other person's asking for. After all, they are presenting me with their problem so they clearly want a solution. And offering help feels good, it increases our sense of happiness and self-esteem. But no matter how tempting it is to come up with a solution to someone else's problems, it's a temptation you should resist.[4]

The tendency or reflex to give advice, offer help or share our own experience may feel good, but it's one of the key factors that prevents us from asking great questions. In the end, the other person is better off finding the answer for themselves. An answer that does justice to their own core values and their sense of what life is all about. It's hard to get these things straight in your own head sometimes. You need someone else for that. Not someone who is brimming with well-intentioned advice, but someone who asks you the right questions – ones that help you think more clearly.

I had the same thing! (Only worse)

Some people have a gift for hijacking a conversation. There you are, just back from your holiday in the Maldives and dying to tell people about it. You take a deep breath, ready to share everything you've done and seen, when the other person wades in and enthusiastically takes over the conversation: 'Oh, the Maldives, that's where we went on our honeymoon! So beautiful! We took a round-trip to several islands and ...'

There is no greater frustration in a conversation than someone who hijacks your story, launches into their own parallel story and rabbits on about it endlessly. Sometimes they even 'one-up' you: 'The Maldives? Oh, that's nothing! We went halfway around the world when we got married. We got to see everywhere from Chile to Costa Rica and Cuba. Had the time of our lives!'

Here too, the path to conversational hell is often paved with good intentions. We slip into the 'I reflex' to let the other person know we share their enthusiasm, and are eager to back it up with similar experiences of our own. Our aim is to forge a bond, to show them we're on the same wavelength. But we achieve the exact opposite: disappointment, irritation and the likelihood that the other person will simply abandon the conversation.

To sum up, we very often fall short in asking questions because of our conversational reflexes. As soon as someone presents us with a narrative, explains a personal problem or asks a question, we are only too happy to advise, offer help or chime in with our own experiences in a similar vein. We are more concerned with ourselves than with the person we're talking to. We want to connect, convince them we're on their side, and we pull out all the stops in the process. Ironically, our performance means they don't feel remotely seen or heard and are much more likely to lose interest. And in the worst instance they may well think twice before ever striking up a conversation with us again.

Asking questions doesn't feel good – talking about yourself does

It shouldn't come as a surprise that we are so quick to throw our own views into the conversation and think about ourselves, even when the other person is talking. In fact there's a very logical explanation: it feels good! Literally.

Research has shown that we talk about ourselves 60 per cent of the time.[5] And if we look at our exchanges on social media – on Twitter or Facebook, for example – that figure shoots up to 80 per cent. It seems there are few things we enjoy more than telling the world what annoys us, gets us down or makes us happy. We wax lyrical about our successes, and make a meal of our complaints. With ourselves as the star of the show: me, myself and I.

There is also a solid biological explanation for this: research shows that talking about yourself – what is on your mind, sharing personal information – causes your brain to produce dopamine, a chemical that gives you a wonderful feeling of intoxication.

Scientists at Harvard University looked into this phenomenon.[6] In an experiment carried out using an fMRI scanner, they asked 195 subjects to discuss their own opinions and character traits, as well as those of others. They then looked at the differences in neurological activity between what the participants said about themselves (self-focused elements) and said about others (other-focused elements).

Three areas of the brain stood out. As expected, and in line with previous research, self-disclosure (talking about yourself) generated higher levels of activity in the medial prefrontal cortex, an area generally associated with thinking about yourself. However, two other areas also lit up in this experiment – areas never previously associated with this type of thinking: the nucleus accumbens and the ventral tegmental area. Both are part of the mesolimbic dopamine system, which is linked to reward responses and the pleasurable feelings associated with stimuli such as sex, cocaine or good food.

The fact that these brain systems are activated when you talk about yourself suggests that self-disclosure, sharing your own story, talking about yourself, is as intrinsically enjoyable as having sex, getting high or stuffing your face. It explains why people are naturally motivated to talk more about themselves than about other topics, however interesting those other topics may be. Talking about yourself is – by nature – simply much more enjoyable. And it provides you with other, more immediate benefits (that delicious dopamine high!) than asking questions.

Socrates would contend that our own story is not really all that interesting. For him, the truly intense and enriching conversations are to be found in what other people are thinking, in exploring those other convictions and events. Becoming wiser is a joint endeavour, and another person's mind is the place where *you* can find new insights.

A philosophy professor of mine once made an interesting distinction between 'opinions' and 'ideas' in a class he was teaching. He proposed that opinions need to belong to someone; that they are views we make our own. If they are questioned, it feels as if we ourselves are being questioned, albeit indirectly. Ideas, on the other hand, don't belong to anybody. An idea is exactly that: an idea. It's something that is open to discussion. You can question an idea, challenge it, kick it about a bit. When you exchange ideas, you enter into conversation on an equal footing. You exchange insights, ask questions and become wiser together.

Ask yourself:
- Now that you've read about these conversational pitfalls, which ones do you recognise in yourself? Do you have a tendency to give advice? To talk about yourself?
- Next time, try to pay closer attention: What effect does helping, advising and taking over the conversation have on your conversations and the person you are talking to? Are they energised or discouraged?
- How do you feel when someone jumps in with unsolicited advice when you are talking to them?
- How do you react when someone pits their own experiences against your own?

REASON TWO: FEAR OF ASKING

Questions are scary

When I interviewed people about asking questions, one of the questions I asked was 'What makes you decide not to ask a question?' The answers I received are ones we can all identify with.

When it comes to asking questions, we are afraid of three things:

1. Making the other person feel uncomfortable
2. The pain and uneasiness we are likely to feel ourselves
3. Conflicts, clashes and general unpleasantness.

I remember listening to a podcast by interviewer Anne Neijnens in which she asked the writer Jan Geurtz how many relationships he was currently in.[7] Not as strange a question as it might seem: she knew that Geurtz took a broad view of monogamy and sometimes had several relationships at the same time. Geurtz refused to answer what he thought was 'far too personal a question' and Anne was left feeling deeply ashamed about asking it. Yet at the same time she felt sure that the answer would be of real interest to her listeners, especially since the entire interview centred on relationships, love, conflicts, monogamy and everything that goes with it.

Sigrid van Iersel, a storyteller and interviewer, is no stranger to this fear of asking certain types of questions:

The hardest thing about asking questions is anticipating how the other person might react. And wondering whether your question might embarrass them. Or being afraid to confront them with something they might be ashamed of. Or with something very personal. The questions that embarrass me most are personal questions that touch on some kind of vulnerability. Is it okay to ask a man with a clear disability about what he can no longer do, or what he misses most? Do I dare ask a woman who can barely read and write if she would like to see the written transcript of our interview? After all, isn't she practically illiterate? Eventually I did ask, but it felt uncomfortable. And that discomfort was more mine than hers. She had long since overcome her shame about her linguistic handicap. Asking about vulnerabilities remains a difficult issue. We project our own notions of shame onto the other person, worry that they will find the topic uncomfortable or perhaps confrontational. It speaks to our own vulnerability. I know I would blame myself if I didn't judge it right. And so I end up not asking the question. Yet at the same time it feels like a missed opportunity.[8]

Sigrid hits the nail on the head. We are afraid to ask pertinent, yet potentially awkward questions that might make someone feel uncomfortable. Yet often these are the very questions that lead to a genuine connection, because so much of what matters in life is located in that vulnerable zone. We're too quick to assume that someone will be reluctant to respond to a particular question.

*

Your own discomfort – or fear of it – can be another reason for swallowing certain questions. Around major life events, such as birth, death and illness, there are issues that can be too painful and personal to touch on. And these can lead you to tread lightly and hold back your questions. Addressing subjects such as cancer or bereavement can feel very different when you have recently lost someone dear or have received an unwelcome diagnosis. There is nothing strange about that, of course. It is understandable that you might not feel brave enough to ask questions under those circumstances, for fear of triggering your own pain, discomfort or even tears.

About eight years ago, before my own search for philosophical questioning began, I learned an important personal lesson when I avoided asking a question out of fear. At the time I was working as a horse trainer and riding instructor, and one of my pupils was Caroline, a lovely girl with whom I got on very well. She owned a beautiful mare, untrained, and we started working with her together. We saw each other almost every week for a session. But then I didn't hear from her for a while. A whole summer passed before she sent me a message to tell me that her father had died suddenly, two months previously. This was the reason she had not kept in touch. Of course I sent her my condolences and wished her all the best. But when we met a few weeks later for a session, I didn't have the nerve to ask her about her father.

I found it too awkward, too uncomfortable to raise the subject, and told myself that Caroline would probably prefer to focus on working with her horse without me stirring up her grief. She later told me she was very sad that I hadn't asked her about her father. Because we got on so well, she had felt the need to share her feelings with me, but found me apparently incurious. I learned a very important lesson that day: not to let my own discomfort and pain be my guide as to whether or not to ask a question.

We'd rather not rock the boat

Agreeing is safer than disagreeing. Differences of opinion are scary. They come with the fear of rejection, of exclusion. The last thing anyone wants is to be shunned by the group, for whatever reason, and an opinion that deviates from the norm is as powerful a reason as any. Maybe that's why we are inclined to make concessions when it comes to our own beliefs.

A young woman who attended one of my 'Critical Thinking' courses summed up this tendency perfectly: 'When I'm asked for an opinion, I usually just wait and see. I'll listen carefully and see what others have to say. It's only when I know what everyone else is thinking that I dare to form my own opinion.'

Before you know it, you've gone along with an opinion that you honestly don't share, and later that same evening you sit there on the sofa feeling annoyed with yourself for not saying what was really on your mind.

The mood in a group is generally at its best when we all agree with one another. When we're celebrating a birthday, we'd rather not get into a heated debate and so we unconsciously reinforce that sense of unity and harmony in the group by asking 'soft' but safe questions. Our need for harmony and affirmation of our own values and beliefs leads us to ask questions designed to steer others towards a socially acceptable response for whatever group of people we find ourselves in. It's a way of trying to keep things friendly.

Asking questions when it comes to matters of race, politics, religion, #MeToo or the climate crisis also comes with a risk attached. These topics are flooded with emotions, personal experiences, political views and private agendas. A conversation might start with something innocent like an article someone has read and, before you know it, suddenly the discussion has got a lot more heated. Then you run the risk of that heated debate developing into a full-blown argument, which might lead to the slamming of doors, yelling things you might later regret or even worse: silence. Long, long silences.

I think it's important for us to be able to engage in these sorts of tough conversations. Later on in the book I will help you develop your questioning and conversational skills, so that when sensitive topics like these are brought to the table, you will know how to discuss them in a calm, considered and open-minded Socratic way.

Asking good questions – open, sincere, curious questions – is a leap of faith: you formulate a question, a genuine question. You send it out into the world and you wait. You don't fill anything in, you don't hope for a particular response or load it with advice. You don't dress it up in opinions and experiences of your own, and you don't approve or disapprove of the other person's answer. And yes, there's a risk that the other person will disagree with you and that the friendly conversation you were having will take an awkward turn for the worse.

A question can knock a person off-balance and introduce tension into a conversation. You might feel shame at having asked a 'rude' question or feel guilty for unsettling the other person. But there's no need for guilt or shame if we handle those questions differently. Without meaning to, we make things very difficult for ourselves as a society: we often blame the questioner for our own discomfort. We tell our kids, 'You mustn't ask that!' We label certain questions 'improper', 'impolite' or 'far too personal'. Or we fob someone off with a curt answer and a comment that 'It's a bit inappropriate to ask that kind of thing'. And if you go ahead and ask that edgy but sincere question, you run the risk of being judged for it. The resulting shame is something we would rather not experience, never mind repeat, so we skirt around questions that might dig a little deeper and take someone out of their comfort zone. The very questions that hold the prospect of a good conversation and a sincere connection. We have created a culture of questioning in which we'd rather not ask the good questions than run the risk of censure: we have created a culture of not-questioning.

It's a strange paradox. When we don't dare to ask questions because our beliefs, vulnerability or a fear of rejection or causing upset get in the way, we are left with only one option: we make assumptions. We fill in the answers for other people, based on our own experiences. We decide what they must be thinking or feeling. What choice do we have? After all, if you don't allow yourself to ask the questions that matter, you don't have much else to go on.

Ask yourself:
- When do you *not* ask a question? What are you afraid of? Making the other person feel uncomfortable? Your own fear? Or are you afraid of conflicts or quarrels?
- Have you ever swallowed a question that you really wanted to ask? Do you remember what was behind your decision?
- When do you think you know what the other person must be thinking or feeling? When do you make assumptions without checking them? Can you remember a specific example?

- Do you ever find yourself trying to control the conversation by phrasing a question in a certain way? How can you tell you are doing this?

REASON THREE: SCORING POINTS

Having an opinion is rewarded much more than asking a question

Another reason why we're sometimes reluctant to ask a question when we'd like to is because asking a question isn't designed to make a big impression. Asking a question means you're curious about the answer. It means you want to know, and therefore implies there's something you don't know – at least not yet. Perhaps your question suggests you're in doubt. And to be in doubt isn't seen as all that cool or sexy. Doubting won't score you any points, it doesn't look good on your CV. Doubt is the antithesis of a USP. You can't enjoy the applause or take a victory lap if you're busy asking questions all the time. It won't make you stand out from the crowd, earn you ratings or get you a promotion. Job ads seldom seek a 'skilled doubter who asks quality questions and is outstanding at suspending their judgement'. More often, in today's world, the opposite is in demand: leaders, decision-makers, people who inspire and take control, go-getters, people who know their mind and speak it with confidence.

*

One of the things I wanted to know when writing this book was 'Why does a person sometimes shy away from asking what they want to ask?' One respondent replied, 'Asking a question shows there's something you don't know. I often notice people avoiding questions for that very reason. Apparently we'd rather stay ignorant than appear stupid.'

We are all too ready to associate 'not-knowing' with 'being an idiot'.

In her book *Braving the Wilderness*, Brené Brown writes:

> I can't remember a time in the last year when someone asked me about an issue and I didn't weigh in with an opinion. Even if I didn't know enough about it to be insightful or even conversational [...] In a fitting-in culture – at home, at work, or in our larger community – curiosity is seen as weakness and asking questions equates to antagonism rather than being valued as learning.[9]

By labelling not-knowing or doubt as inferior, we create an ideal breeding ground for blaring uninformed opinions in place of asking good questions. In an effort to mask our own uncertainty, we try to pass off our coffee-break chit-chat as well-considered analysis. To avoid coming across as doubt-ridden fools, we pretend to know what we're talking about.

Someone who asks questions, someone who has doubts, is unsure. And someone who is unsure isn't worth the time of day. As part of this drive to appear competent, we like to present opinions as facts.

Janine Abbring is a highly respected figure in Dutch broadcasting, a driving force behind the country's most popular and influential satirical current-affairs show, *Sunday with Lubach*. The show made an international splash when its 'video message' to a newly elected Donald Trump – 'America First, Holland Second' – went viral.[10]

With credentials like these, Janine Abbring must have seemed like an ideal guest for the Dutch version of comedy news quiz *Have I Got News For You*.[11] During the show Janine explains that she doesn't really have a watertight opinion about anything, to which the host responds, 'In that case, what are you doing here?'

Fellow panellist and comedian Peter Pannekoek challenges her. 'But you work on *Sunday with Lubach*, a show that goes out of its way to take a stand on all kinds of issues.'

Janine answers, 'Yes, but when we're working on the show it takes us a good while to arrive at that position. That's something I really value.'

At which the rest of the panel weigh in with quips like, 'Tell you what: why don't we all take a toilet break and leave you to have a quiet think about your opinion.'

Later Janine spoke about this experience in an interview with Dutch daily newspaper *de Volkskrant*:

I never form an instant opinion about anything. I often doubt myself. And on that news quiz, the host got really shirty about it. He asked me what I thought about populist politician Thierry Baudet. They were clearly expecting a pithy one-liner because – hey, it's TV after all – but when I'm put on the spot like that my brain just seizes up and all I can come out with is 'Oh, uh, give me a sec because on the one hand I think … uh …' At one point, the host snapped: 'Do you actually know what you think about anything?' It was really uncomfortable.[12]

The TV quizmaster's impatience is far from exceptional. Voicing an outspoken opinion in order to fit in, or appear witty, has crept into the heart of our culture and has virtually become a precondition for participating in the public debate at all. Stating that opinion in the strongest possible terms is seen as infinitely preferable to doubt or silence. Yet at the same time it's worth asking what this actually contributes to the well-being of society. Changing your opinion is seen as a weakness, yet that is the very essence of 'agile perspective'.

Doubt is not something we like to cultivate. Traditionally we like to be sure, to know where we stand. Human beings don't exactly thrive on doubt, on not having a ready-made and comforting truth to hand. Our brains don't know quite how to cope with open endings. And a question, especially one that remains unanswered, is an open ending of sorts.

Our need to resolve this tension is the reason why TV cliff-hangers work so well. There's no better way to keep people watching than by ratcheting up the stakes towards the end of an episode and delivering a final shot that leaves everything wide open. Will our hero save the day? Is that young stranger really her long-lost son? Broadcasters and streaming services by the score make a mint from unanswered questions and open endings, because we long to see them satisfyingly resolved.

In the good old days of hunter-gathering, when we used to lurk in the bushes with stone-tipped spears and ambush wild animals, rapid answers were exactly what we needed. Skills like knowing where to find food quickly, and the best way to kill and prepare it, were vital to our survival. The last thing we needed as a prehistoric human struggling to survive was a question. In that sense, we humans are not programmed 'not to know'. We seem to be hard-wired for something snappier than taking time to reflect on a question or explore an important issue.

The second that I ask, 'What time is it?' or 'What's for dinner tonight?', you start looking for the answer. It's what the brain does. It searches for the required information, forges links between facts, analyses what it can or can't do with them and moves on to the next step. Amid the practicalities of everyday life, answering questions quickly is a very useful ability. But we also apply this same tendency to the bigger questions that don't always lend themselves to snappy, unequivocal answers. Should I change careers? Would we be happier if we got divorced? Am I a good person?

Because we are so accustomed to searching for – and finding – answers quickly, that's also our reflex when it comes to life's major quandaries. But when faced with fundamental disagreements, judgements or life choices, that reflex can work against us. In situations like that, you sometimes simply have to face up to not-knowing.

Question makers – not opinion leaders

An entire profession has arisen from our desire to score points by voicing opinions: the opinion leader. Opinion leaders are people who adopt a viewpoint and shout it from the rooftops with the aim of encouraging other people to think the same way they do. They bombard each other with opinions and often demonstrate all the flexibility of a block of concrete. 'Opinion leader' strikes me as a strange term. In a way they're almost our prompters, feeding us lines when we have none. Apparently, we need prompting. Have we forgotten how to think autonomously and form well-founded, nuanced opinions of our own?

Opinion leaders can provide a sharp focus. They can pep up our thinking and make us see things in a different light. But pit one hard-nosed opinion against another and you create the perfect conditions for polarisation. Any sense of nuance is banished to the margins, left to take one last disappointed look around before slinking off into the shadows. This battle of ready-made opinions also makes us lazy: we can just sit back and pick whichever one we like. And when another wordsmith finds an even more appealing way to express the opposite view, we may switch sides just as readily. Like picking out a new jacket, we try on different opinions and see how they fit. Perhaps there's a little bit of my own opinions or beliefs in there somewhere, but mostly it's the work of a bunch of other people who have been doing all my thinking for me.

Given the speed at which opinions are launched into the public arena nowadays, people no longer have ample room to order their own thoughts. In the time it takes to make yourself a cup of tea, a brand-new opinion can blast its way into your brain. Rob Wijnberg, founder of the alternative news platform The Correspondent, neatly sums up the frantic pace of things: 'It usually takes [...] a few hours at most for any news item to be furnished with commentary by a whole army of politicians, opinion leaders and journalists, often before it's even clear exactly what has happened or what's been said.'[13]

The ability to say 'I don't know' and keep your mouth shut while you take some quiet time to come up with a carefully formulated question might be every bit as necessary as the views trumpeted by opinion leaders.

Maybe it's time to introduce a whole new profession to the media landscape: question makers. People who are happy to admit they don't know yet, who are more focused on asking questions that help us develop our thinking than in formulating the answers. Question makers who start a school of thought that invites calm contemplation and reflection. Question makers who don't put forward a proposition, but who explore an issue in a spirit of enquiry. Who ask questions that make you think, questions that invite others to engage in conversation. Questions that are meant to deepen, clarify, develop new perspectives.

These question makers can make regular appearances on panel discussions and chat shows. They can write columns in Sunday supplements. With the sole purpose of supplying viewers and readers with questions that provide food for thought, in the conviction that a good question sets things in motion, while an answer stops people thinking.

In my ideal world, chat-happy TV hosts would finally master the pregnant pause and let their interviewees think before they speak. They would be silent and swallow their so-called 'questions-that-aren't-really-questions'. What would the world be like if our TV shows, newspapers and influencers became question makers? Perhaps then we could get by with fewer clashes and interruptions, and find more space for difficult and productive conversations.

Philosophers sometimes fulfil that role, and since 2011 the Netherlands has had the philosophical equivalent of a poet laureate – a thinker laureate – to offer the country keen questions and new ways of thinking, someone who can place our fast-paced news cycle in a larger context. But you don't have to hold a degree in philosophy or be a philosophical laureate to become a question maker. As far as I'm concerned, the world needs far more question makers than that.

Ask yourself:
- Do you recognise these tendencies in yourself?
- Do you ever express an opinion before you've thought it through, for the sake of making an impression?
- Do you have the courage, like Janine Abbring, to say you don't know or haven't formed an opinion on a burning issue of the day?

REASON FOUR: LACK OF OBJECTIVITY

Our ability to reason objectively is in decline

In a society where opinions are as valuable as facts, objectivity automatically fades into the background. This is another reason why we no longer ask questions and why, when we do, they often lack focus. We like to insist that everyone has the right to their own truth. 'Well, that's your opinion and you're entitled to it.' Or 'You've got your truth and I've got mine.' It's a defining element of our outlook on life these days: everyone has their own truth, one that needs to be taken very seriously indeed.

This personal truth, enshrined in our opinions, goes on to form our identity, and that's something we don't like to call into question. Never mind being flexible enough to review our views and opinions. Objectivity? Uh ... what was that again?

In an interview with the Dutch national daily *Trouw*, philosopher Daan Roovers said:

> People think that every statement you make or prejudice you express deserves special protection. I think that's a major misunderstanding. Freedom of expression is a political right accorded to citizens in their relationship with the government. Not to children in relation to their parents or citizens in relation to each other. And that freedom includes a willingness to question your own opinion and to accept criticism from others. *That* is the nature of the public debate.[14]

Once an opinion has been formed, it's a difficult thing to shrug off, even in the face of compelling arguments. Recent research has shown that people cling to their opinions even more tightly when confronted with evidence to the contrary.

In his books, Flemish philosopher and biologist Ruben Mersch investigates how this works by looking at a number of psychological experiments. They include the following thought experiment by Jonathan Haidt of New York University, a specialist in moral psychology:

> Julie and Mark, who are sister and brother, are travelling together in France. They are both on summer vacation from college. One night they are staying alone in a cabin near the beach. They decide that it would be interesting and fun if they tried making love. At the very least it would be a new experience for each of them. Julie is already taking birth control pills, but Mark uses a condom too, just to be safe. They both enjoy it, but they decide not to do it again. They keep that night as a special secret between them, which makes them feel even closer to each other.[15]

Haidt presented this situation to a range of people and asked them what they thought of Julie and Mark's behaviour. Everyone disapproved and labelled it wrong or immoral, but none of them could produce a convincing argument to support their point of view. Objectively speaking, no crime had been committed and there was no danger of inbreeding. Brother and sister both consented and did no harm to anyone. In other words, the convictions expressed by the respondents were not based on knowledge or facts, but purely on instinct.

Using this and other examples, Mersch demonstrates that our gut feeling usually wins out over reason. People continue to defend their own point of view, feelings or beliefs, even when the facts and figures contradict their judgement. 'We tend to use facts like a drunk uses a lamppost,' he writes. 'Not for illumination, but simply for support.' We are always looking to be proven right and so we filter the information we encounter in ways that suit our own point of view. 'We don't question reality, we torture her until she confesses what we want to hear,' Mersch writes.[16]

In another of his books Mersch considers an experiment that involves an fMRI scan, which measures brain activity and can register what happens in the brain when we have an emotional response. Now, imagine three test subjects. The first receives an almighty slap. Not surprisingly, the scan will register quite a strong emotional response. The second is subjected to all manner of verbal abuse. Their scan will differ very little from the first. The third person is bombarded with arguments that are diametrically opposed to their most deeply held convictions. And guess what: the third scan shows the same result. A slap, verbal abuse or an unwelcome opinion: to your brain, it's all the same. You aren't thinking rationally; you are in survival mode.[17]

Asking questions – sincere and curious questions – could well mean having to revise our own opinions. And everything in us resists doing exactly that. We'd rather be secure in our wrongful convictions than in a state of justifiable uncertainty. At an instinctive level, a challenging question sends us hurtling into survival mode because it poses a threat to our identity.

Of course this doesn't apply to factual questions like 'Where do you live?' But it's hard to avoid feeling at least a little agitated when someone decides to question your statements and expects you to explain why you said what you said:

Statement:	'I just don't believe in hierarchies. I mean, everyone's capable of taking their own responsibility, aren't they? Hierarchical organisations just don't work.'
Question:	'Why don't hierarchical organisations work?'
Statement:	'I have nothing against homosexuality. Nothing at all. I just don't want to be confronted with it.'
Question:	'So can you explain what is it about homosexuality that means you don't want to be confronted with it?'

Cognitive neuroscientist Tali Sharot had this to say on the subject, in an interview with the Dutch daily *Trouw*:

Our beliefs are part of who we are. Information that goes against them threatens the core of our personality.

And so we resist it. We don't want to question our beliefs and who we are. Young children believe their parents if they say they saw a pink elephant flying through the sky, because to young children the world is still completely new. They have often noticed that very strange things turn out to be possible. But adults have strong beliefs that cannot easily be shaken. And in many cases, that's justified. On the whole, our assumptions are correct: there is gravity, the sun rises and sets, there are no pink elephants flying around. That mechanism makes it very difficult to change unjustified beliefs.[18]

When you are asked a question, the obligation to come up with an answer means you have to think. Basically that means you are being invited, or even challenged, to review or reformulate your current position, reformulate your opinion or admit that you are just plain wrong. You are being invited to train yourself in 'agile perspective'. And making room for objectivity means daring to let go of the assertion 'This is my truth'.

One of the first Socratic discussions I was involved in centred on the question 'Is your love for your children unconditional?' Six people took part and more than half agreed that, yes, love between parents and children is unconditional. One of them, Sarah, was particularly outspoken in her view: 'I have two kids and I just know that I will always love them.

No matter what they do, that love will remain. Come what may. Always.'

Another member of the group wanted to question her about this deeply held conviction. 'How can you be so sure that your love will remain, no matter what they do?'

'Look … I just *know*!'

A third participant asked, 'What if one of your children killed someone in a fit of rage? Would your love be just as strong?'

'Well, uh … that's such a weird example!' she began to respond, indignantly. 'I mean, what am I supposed to say to that?'

Putting up with being questioned, enduring being challenged, accepting the invitation to consider things more deeply, to reflect on and sometimes even scrutinise what we say or think: all these things make us anxious and we prefer to avoid them when we can. After all, we largely derive our identity from our beliefs and convictions. Behind our statements and opinions lies an entire view of the world and human nature. No wonder it feels like there's a lot at stake if we are made to step back and reassess. The reflex is to protect what you know. Not so much the specific view you have just expressed, but the greater underlying conviction that stands for your whole identity at that moment.

In this case, when pressed on her opinion, Sarah avoided answering the question and reacted defensively. She clearly had no desire to take a critical look at her rock-solid conviction, to question her own truth. She didn't even want to consider the possibility that her love for her children might not be as unconditional as she had thought. Yet the purpose of philosophising is to face up to questions like these. Eventually she did, although she had to dig deep. Someone else put the question to her again, as calmly as possible: 'Imagine a situation in which one of your children murdered someone for no apparent, defensible reason. Would your love for your child remain as strong, or would it change?'

She went quiet for a moment, winced, shifted uncomfortably in her seat and eventually sighed, 'No, if I'm honest, I think that in that scenario my love would change. And that there might be something conditional about it after all.'

Ask yourself:
- When do you react defensively?
- Are you open to facts that chip away at your views and undermine your truth? Or do you find that difficult?
- Think back to a question that made you feel uncomfortable: what didn't you want to face up to at the time? What were you defending or protecting?
- Have you ever asked a question that made another person react defensively, or made them feel uncomfortable or angry? What conviction do you think they were trying to protect?

REASON FIVE: IMPATIENCE

We think asking good questions is a waste of time (and time is in short supply)

Another interesting response to my query 'What stops you asking a question?' came from an activities coach in the care sector.

'There are times when I don't ask questions either, and mostly it's because I know how busy people are ... or think they are! They don't seem to have the patience for a good conversation or to go into detail if you ask a question. These days it's all about short, sharp answers and stating your own opinion, whereas asking questions calls for a completely different attitude. Ask a good question and there's every chance you'll be dismissed as an oddball, someone who's stuck in the past. There's no time – or, rather, a lot of people don't take the time – to explore an issue in depth. And that involves asking good questions.'

I think they're right. We no longer have, and no longer take, the time to explore. Our urge is to move on as swiftly as possible. That reassuring feeling we get from thinking we know things for sure is compounded by our sense that a sincere, curious exploration of what we think we know is surplus to requirements. Who needs to get bogged down in a time-consuming process when we're busy enough as it is? And so we leave well enough alone. We labour under the misapprehension that a good conversation eats into our time, when in fact it usually saves us time. How much miscommunication could be avoided? How many failed projects and collaborative mismatches would turn out differently if everyone took the time to come together and look into things in a little more depth, to ask a few more questions and enter into some collective reflection on the essentials?

Ariane van Heijningen is a practical philosopher and organisational strategist who founded her own agency called DENKPLAATS, which means, quite literally, 'a place to think'. She told me about the thoughtful discussions that she facilitates within organisations, and that the first step is always to identify the exact nature of the problem. She has seen situations where the executive board or the management team thinks the problem is somewhere that it's really not. Turnover is too low, for example, and it immediately goes hunting for solutions, launches a campaign to attract investors – you name it. But sometimes that's not where the problem lies at all. Maybe the organisation needs to have another kind of discussion first.

It might be that an element of the company culture has gone awry. Or that a once-popular product is failing to move with the times. Or something else entirely. But why tear around trying to come up with solutions without first being clear about the exact nature of the problem? When an organisation decides to team up with a practical philosopher like Ariane, that's what they are trying to find. By having discussions that are designed to help it think things through. Using systematic questioning, such as the Socratic method, she works to bring the real question, the real problem, to the fore:

> In a Socratic discussion, you apply logic in an attempt to uncover the real story, to pinpoint the moments when people contradict themselves or each other, to identify hidden presuppositions and open them up to discussion. That gives you the opportunity to take a different view and make different decisions. In my experience, people are happy to have this kind of discussion because it gives them room to think. Which is not to say it's easy, or that it's a quick fix. If you remain curious and try to get to the bottom of things together, it can take a little while but nine times out of ten you end up with a better and more efficient decision. Ultimately, the time you invest pays off in the time you save.[19]

Conducting a thoughtful discussion or dialogue not only takes time – it also requires discipline. And that tends to be in short supply. We often blame our habits on lack of time: we simply have too little of it to enter into a good conversation and ask a well-considered question. But more often than not, it's actually discipline that's lacking. Not that there is any need for blame, either. How are you supposed to be disciplined in something you've never practised? Nevertheless, this lack of discipline is still another key cause of the shallowness of our conversations and the absence of good questions driving those conversations.

Take your time – lots of time – and ask a different question

Not so long ago, in collaboration with two fellow practitioners, I held a philosophical discussion with the directors and governors of a healthcare institution. They were keen to engage in a philosophical exploration of their new core values: courage, wonder and trust. Because they wanted to do more than talk, we devised an experiential exercise relating to each core value. The participants' experiences would then provide the ingredients for a Socratic discussion.

I gave them the following exercise: in no more than two sentences, write down something that annoyed or irritated you in the past few weeks. We then split into pairs. One participant read out their irritation, while the other had to listen in silence for a full minute. After this silence, the listener was permitted to ask a single question. The answer wasn't important. What mattered was the experience of hearing a story, knowing that you are going to ask a question and having to take a minute to think about it.

The result was fascinating: the minute's silence felt a little uncomfortable at first and there was some giggling.

But within seconds, giggles made way for concentration. At the end of the exercise, the pairs exchanged experiences and every one of the participants said the question they asked at the end of the minute was very different from the one that had first come to mind.

When asked to compare their initial question with the one they actually asked, they unfailingly described the one-minute question as the better of the two. As one participant put it, 'The first questions that popped into my head weren't all that interesting. If I'm honest, they were skewed towards a particular answer or more for my own amusement. But the question that came to my mind after the minute's silence really got to the heart of the matter and made my partner think.'

Although we often jump to the conclusion that asking good questions takes time, it's just as true to say that taking the time to formulate a good question saves you time. The quality of the question – and therefore the answer – improves, the more attention you pay to it. Or as the old saying goes, if you want to speed up, slow down.

Ask yourself:
- Do you just assume that asking questions takes time?
- When are you inclined to jump the gun?
- When do you make do with a quick fix instead of asking questions that matter?

REASON SIX: LACK OF COMPETENCE

Nobody teaches us how

I used to be a regular question machine. A persistent little gadfly who kept buzzing away until she got an answer. One of those kids who's always asking 'Why?' and drives their parents up the wall.

'Mummy, why is there a big balloon in the sky?'

'Because people like balloons and they want to see the world from up high.'

'Why do people want to see the world from up high?'

'Because they like the way it looks, I suppose.'

'So can we do that? Go up in a big balloon?'

'We can, but we're not going to.'

'Why aren't we going to, if we can?'

'Well … uh … because I said so!'

I seldom settled for the obvious answer. Behind every question I asked, another question was ready for take-off. I wanted the answers behind, above, beside and below the first one I was given. When the interrogation had gone on long enough, my parents regularly resorted to that old chestnut 'Because I said so.' It's an all-purpose way to give your child the brush-off and pre-empt endless conversations. And it's a not-so-subtle message to children that asking questions is not necessarily appreciated. Understandable, of course. It takes both time and patience to humour a child's inquisitive nature, to cherish and nurture their enquiring minds. But it's worth it. Worth putting in the time, both to answer them sincerely and to ask questions of your own that keep your children thinking and fire up their imaginations.

Thinking flexibly, having an inquisitive attitude, examining a theme or subject from all sides and working out the answers: all these things come naturally to children, but plant them in our modern-day education system and those promising young shoots soon wither away. From primary school through high school, college and university and on to working life – apart from a handful of noble efforts and worthy initiatives, such as lessons in philosophy or critical thinking for children – asking questions and adopting a philosophical, enquiring attitude are far from the norm. I've yet to encounter a primary school that consistently teaches the art of thinking and asking questions, yet surely this is a key life skill? The ability to think critically, to question our own and other people's views and to adopt multiple perspectives produces keen-minded adults who know how to better connect with one another. And we need these people now more than ever.

Some schools pour their resources into art projects to get children thinking creatively, or put philosophical reasoning on their curriculum. But even then, the going can be tough. Teachers often find that to conduct a genuinely enquiring discussion in the classroom, they have to abandon the role they have been trained to fulfil: someone who oversees the teaching of a curriculum and is meant to provide students with the right answers. Melanie Eijdems, who teaches ten- to twelve-year olds, came along to one of my 'Philosophising in the Classroom' workshops, designed for teachers in the final years of primary school. She told me:

> As a teacher, you are mainly trained to ask questions that elicit knowledge. By testing your pupils' knowledge, you can see whether they've understood the lesson. It's only in the past few years that more attention has been paid to questions that tap into pupils' abilities to think critically.

In all likelihood, this new trend stems from the current focus on 'twenty-first-century skills', one of which is critical thinking.[20]

Melanie feels that this activity takes a lot of practice, especially for more established teachers who are not used to thinking and working that way:

> As a teacher, I do ask genuinely open questions, but they are more to do with personal things. How's your grandma doing now? How does that make you feel? What can I do for you? Asking similar questions in the context of a specific lesson can be tricky. It means putting aside my role as 'overseer' and being genuinely curious about the answers my pupils come up with.

Melanie's account is very similar to other stories that I hear from teachers when I give workshops and training courses at primary schools. First they have to contend with the traditions of the teaching profession – traditions that have been in place for years. And on top of that comes pressure of work, scrutiny from school inspectors and parental expectations, all of which limit the scope for creativity and good conversations.

Her dealings with parents have made Melanie realise just how much society focuses on knowledge rather than creativity or thinking skills. Parents, like the school inspectors, are primarily focused on results. There are parents who practically demand that their child is placed in the highest-achieving levels of secondary education, and who see it as a failure of the teacher if a school's more realistic assessment doesn't live up to their own ambitions for their child. As Melanie says:

Where, for example, the early-childhood teacher once had time to observe a child and offer them resources to develop in various creative areas, now parents in the playground boast that 'my six-year-old can already read, write, add and subtract'. The fact that 'my eight-year-old daughter sings like an angel or loves drawing' doesn't seem relevant at all. The higher demands set by many parents and society as a whole often mean that lessons that call for skills other than arithmetic, reading comprehension and spelling end up being dismissed by many parents as simply 'messing about'. Yet messing about and having lively, open discussions are the very things that enable children to develop enquiring minds and creative attitudes.

I once gave a course in 'Creativity and Critical Thinking' at a primary school. The assignment I gave the teachers was to devise and facilitate a creative process for their pupils. The goal was to give their pupils full ownership of their own process, thinking and choices. In short, the kids had to work autonomously, based on a theme. Ellen, a Year 8 teacher, said, 'In my class, there's a huge emphasis on "winning or losing". This has a negative impact on how the children interact at playtime. I'd like to show them that winning or losing doesn't matter, and that you can just have fun together regardless. That's what I'd like to do in this creative class. Is that okay?'

During another training session, on philosophical discussions in the classroom, a religious studies teacher confessed, 'I had a class discussion on the question "Can you only pray in a place of worship?" But I couldn't help myself and towards the end I began sharing my own views on the subject. Because I honestly believe that's how they should also think about prayer.'

Even when it comes to philosophy or art, teachers tend to steer and exert control over the ideas that emerge during a class. They have great difficulty letting go and granting the children autonomy, and almost feel a responsibility to express their own views. This is reinforced by the fact that the children aren't used to having that degree of freedom and often say things like 'But you'll give us the right answer in a minute, won't you, Miss?'

The way in which we organise our education systems has a huge effect on our children's ability to think for themselves, whether they are able to adopt an inquisitive attitude or dare to ask questions. If anything, the majority of education today is more about curtailing that ability than developing it.

Teacher-training courses do not train prospective teachers in questioning skills, either. Anne Baudine, a teacher-in-training, told me during a 'Critical Thinking' workshop at her school, 'Philosophy is part of my teacher-training programme, but it mostly boils down to a historical overview of philosophers and their ideas. As for how to actually hold an in-depth discussion, let alone get my pupils to come up with their own questions … I have no idea.'

The lack of questioning skills and an open, inquisitive attitude in primary schools is also felt in higher education and in the workforce. There, too, theory and knowledge often take centre stage, while not enough emphasis is given to training and developing an enquiring, learning attitude. Yet all the time the need for these skills is growing.

Professor Jan Bransen, philosopher and behavioural scientist at Radboud University in the Netherlands, is a passionate advocate of educational reform. He argues that education's current emphasis on acquiring and testing knowledge is based on the notion that knowledge and its application are two different things. In Bransen's view, knowledge is only real knowledge when it can be expressed as professional action in any circumstances and is not limited to situations X or Y. To enable this type of knowledge acquisition, education needs to focus on three things: socialisation, personal development and qualification. Bransen believes it is crucial that, in a world where so many sources of information are available, young people learn to critically evaluate that information and distinguish between opinion and fact. This capacity to think critically is insufficiently trained and nurtured by our present education system, which is still overly obsessed with knowledge transfer and how to assess it.[21]

Ask yourself:
- Thinking back to your upbringing and your school days, what values did you absorb when it came to asking questions? Was asking questions appreciated and stimulated? Or was it discouraged?

Understanding the reasons why you don't ask questions can help you do things differently. When you know that you are being held back by fear or ego, it becomes easier to recognise and alter that dynamic in yourself. When you realise that you're spouting an opinion for the sake of making an impression when you'd really rather ask a question, this awareness can help you do things differently the next time around. And when you understand that asking the right questions will *save* rather than waste your time, you are more likely to take the plunge.

But awareness is only part of the puzzle. Once you know why you avoid asking questions, or why you ask such lousy questions, and decide you want to better your ways – where do you start? That's what the next part of this book is all about: the basics of the Socratic attitude and the foundation for asking good questions. Once you begin to strengthen that attitude, then rewarding and relevant questions will come much more naturally than they did before.

PART TWO

PART TWO

The Socratic attitude

Wisdom is like a baobab tree: no one individual can embrace it.

Ghanaian proverb

From slouch to superhero: awakening your inner Socrates

INSIDE ME LIVES a mini-Socrates. He wears a Batman cape that flaps in the breeze, and he occasionally gets a little too fanatical about saving the world and finds himself running headlong into a brick wall. Hence my inner Socrates has a permanent plaster stuck to his nose.

Everyone has a little Socrates inside them. Some are fast asleep or lounge around thoughtlessly picking at their teeth. Others are absorbed in a comic book, engrossed in a video game or tucking into a tub of Ben & Jerry's ice cream. But potentially all these Socrateses are capable of fulfilling their purpose in life: to remain curious and 'not-knowing', ready to challenge and primed to ask probing questions. Succeed in waking up your inner Socrates and you've struck pure gold. Your conversations will offer more fun and fulfilment, and observing the people around you can become more fascinating than your favourite Netflix series.

What we can learn from Socrates and other practical philosophers, such as Epictetus and the Stoics, is how they were able to bring depth to a conversation by asking questions. How they gave people food for thought. They entered into dialogues that went way beyond the standard patchwork of opinions that passes for conversation today. By awakening your own inner Socrates, your conversations will become richer, deeper and maybe even more philosophical.

So what exactly is a Socratic attitude?

Socrates believed that only the man who knows himself, and knows that he knows nothing, has room for true knowledge. In Part One we discovered that one of our biggest problems is our deep-rooted love of answers. Not to mention our readiness to think we know the score, and our fondness for filling in the gaps and making assumptions. The solution – the way to ask better questions – lies in confronting the assumption that we can know something for sure.

Socrates was the very embodiment of a questioning attitude: a perspective defined by wonder, by not-knowing, by an almost fatuous lack of assumptions. For him, no area was off-limits – not even the stuff we usually take for granted, the stuff that seems blindingly obvious. He opened it all up for discussion by asking question after question. It's thinking we know things for sure that stops us asking the questions that matter.

At work, for example, we are all too eager to cooperate with one another, yet organisations seldom take time out to ask: what *is* cooperation? Asking that question, however futile it may seem and however self-evident the answer, nevertheless results in deeper connection and understanding. It reveals that John from Marketing has a completely different view of cooperation than Laura from Finance and Carl from Human Resources. Consult any dictionary you like, but a definition of 'cooperation' as 'joint action or operation'[1] won't get you very far when it comes to considering the practical implications of what cooperation actually means. After all, what form should that 'joint-ness' take? What actions need to be taken, how frequently, for how long and by whom? And how exactly do we feel about 'operating jointly' in the first place?

This questioning, not-knowing attitude comes naturally to children. They are constantly amazed, eager to investigate and ask the most wonderful questions. Because they know there are all kinds of things they don't yet know. You can adopt a questioning attitude towards everything and everyone: yourself, a newspaper article, the news, a juicy piece of gossip. It's an attitude that goes in search of not-knowing, an attitude that can be developed by yourself, for yourself; no one else need be involved.

But how do you go about training this Socratic questioning attitude, which is essentially at odds with what us grown-ups are so used to doing? A questioning attitude is not something you develop overnight, just as you won't shed those extra pounds after a single gym session … if only! To see results you have to train, develop stamina and keep your new-found routine ticking over. The same goes for your mind.

As devotees of yoga and mindfulness like to say, 'It's a practice.' And practice makes perfect. If you want to master something, you have to do it regularly, whether that's training your body or focusing your mind. The Socratic attitude is no different, and conducting thoughtful conversations also requires a bit of practice. Practice takes time, concentration, dedication and putting thoughts into action: to develop a Socratic attitude you have to stick at it.

How do I train a new Socratic attitude?

The first step in developing a questioning Socratic attitude is to be aware of your own thinking: both what you think and how you think. Only then can you steer your thoughts in the right direction, make adjustments where necessary and allow scope for genuine questions. The *what* and the *how* are really two different entities. *What* means discovering the convictions that underlie your thought processes, often without you even realising it. And then there's the *how*. Do you think fast or slow? Associatively or logically? As the Ancient Greeks put it: know thyself. Only when you know what you think, and how you think it, can you consciously shape your thought processes and create space for something else to evolve.

Try to observe your own thoughts as often as you can. The better you get to know your own thinking, the easier it becomes to recognise patterns and break free of them at a later stage. Observe your thinking without judgement. It's no big deal if you find yourself judging others or giving yourself a hard time. Don't worry if your mind goes walkabout in the middle of a conversation, or if you find yourself focusing on your own concerns or making a shopping list. Simply register whatever's happening and bring your attention back to the conversation you're having.

A practical exercise in observing your own thinking

You can observe your own thinking any time you like, only you don't always want to inflict this process on the person you're talking to. Try listening to a radio or TV interview, or observing a conversation between two people without taking part. Be very aware of what you're thinking. What thoughts are going through your head? What judgements are you making? What are those judgements about? What catches your attention? Are you still following the interview or has your attention been grabbed by the argument you had with your friend or thoughts of what you're going to have for dinner tonight? Don't judge your own thinking, simply note what's going on. This furnishes you with information about your own inclinations. Maybe your mind has a tendency to wander or you're itching to respond to what you hear. 'Yes, I'm the same!' 'No, I'd never do that!' Or 'Crikey, what a stupid thing to be worried about!' Training your own thinking and developing a Socratic attitude starts with a clear focus on what you are doing right here and now.

A while back I was driving along in my car, listening to the radio. The presenter was interviewing model Loiza Lamers. Men's lifestyle magazine *FHM* had just released its list of the world's sexiest women, and Loiza was among them. Her first brush with celebrity had come when she became the first transgender woman to win a *Next Top Model* reality show. The interviewer talked about the *FHM* list and asked Loiza how it felt to be ranked as one of the sexiest women in the world. Did she think it was an important moment for other transgender women? Was it her mission to give a voice to the transgender community?

So far, so good. But then he took a deep breath and asked out of nowhere, 'And … uh … What was it like, the first time, having sex as a woman?' I nearly went hurtling into the nearest crash barrier. Alone in the car, I heard myself yelling out loud, 'You moron! What a fucking nerve! What's *that* got to do with anything?' I couldn't remember the last time I got so worked up over a question.

When I took a step back from my own thinking, I was able to analyse my initial thought – 'What an idiotic question!' – and get a handle on my outrage. I was angry because I thought it was a ridiculous question, one I didn't think the interviewer had the right to ask. It smacked of sensationalism. It wasn't a question born of interest or genuine curiosity and it didn't follow on from any part of the preceding conversation. The fact that I got so worked up about it proved to me, more than anything, how important it is that questions should be sincere and geared towards connection, not used to satisfy the lurid curiosity or cynical humour of a potential listener.

Regardless of whether I was right or wrong in my anger, it was a pure and intense moment that allowed me to observe my own thoughts and literally go back through and examine them one by one. It made me wiser. My own split-second judgement put me in touch with my beliefs about the essence of a good conversation: a sincere connection and asking questions that are about the *other* person, and that seek to bring out the story *they* are telling.

*

When awareness of your own thinking settles in, you can slowly start to steer that thinking. When you notice yourself becoming distracted, bring your attention back to the person you're talking to. If you feel yourself becoming caught up in your own world, clear your head and regroup so that you can once again listen attentively to what the other person has to say. If you are catapulted into an emotional reaction or judgement, as I was in the car that day, take a step back and examine the values on which that judgement is based. This calls for a great deal of practice, concentration and discipline, but it is a key condition for asking good questions.

EMBRACING WONDER

If wonder was a character in a story, she would be shy. She would retreat into herself if there was too much chatter going on around her. Faced with fierce stares, cynical sighs and snarky remarks, she'd fall silent. A little too sensitive perhaps, she would take to her heels at the slightest threat from her arch-enemy 'judgement'. She would know what she needed, but wouldn't dare ask for it. Wonder would exist by the grace of the space she's given, not the space she takes up. Which isn't very much at all. When given the time and the space, she settles down in a corner and simply observes. She looks, listens, notices and seeks out the emptiness in herself so that she can meet the other person with the clearest of heads and an open heart.

'Philosophy begins in wonder.' Our hero Socrates said that, too, centuries ago.[2] One of the key elements of a questioning attitude is wonder. As a concept, it's not that easy to describe. The dictionary gives 'great surprise'[3] as a synonym for wonder, but for me there's a subtle difference. You tend to be surprised when there is some degree of shock in a situation – when the last thing you were expecting to happen suddenly does. For example, your unfailingly tardy colleague can surprise you by suddenly turning up for work ten minutes early.

Wonder is more subtle. Wonder is a choice. I can look at exactly the same situation with and without wonder. The choice lies both in the situation and in how I choose to perceive it, whether I do or don't take the whole experience for granted. I am aware that Earth is not the only planet in our solar system, that there are other planets and they all orbit around the sun. I can take that as read or I can choose to contemplate it with a sense of wonder. To appreciate how remarkable it is that all those planets exist, and how small we really are.

When one of my best friends told me she was pregnant, I was struck by wonder. How amazing it was that, even as we spoke, the beginnings of a brand-new life were taking shape inside her. A whole new human being, who will one day grow into an adult and develop their own ideas and character traits along the way. Wonderful, in every sense. Yet you can view exactly the same phenomenon as completely unremarkable: I mean, I've lost count of the number of baby showers I've been to in the past five years.

Another example we can all recognise: clouds. Surely there's not a single person who hasn't at some point lain on their back in the grass and thought, 'Hey, clouds are really quite something. The people in that aeroplane are high above, looking down at them. And I'm way down here, gazing up. And that one over there looks like a crocodile with wings!' Yet there are plenty of other days when we barely stop to give those fluffy balls of wonder a second thought.

That same principle, opting for wonder, can also be applied to everyday situations. Where normally I would be quick to label, pigeonhole or jump to conclusions, I can also choose to look at a situation with wonder. A moment of irritation when spending time with my mother, my partner, a friend – Why are they reacting so emotionally? Why can't we have a normal conversation for once! – can turn into something quite different if I can find a way to look at it with a sincere sense of wonder. Instead of getting caught up in my own judgements, wonder can open the door to genuine questions. What's making my friend lose their temper like that? Can I see the assumptions that underlie their reproaches? And how am I responding to them? What assumptions am I making about this conversation?

Wonder means looking beyond what seems self-evident. It's about wanting to see how special things can be. We can choose to use that sense of wonder, to let it into our lives, to nurture it. Before you know where you are, your day can be packed with too much noise and too many opinions, leaving too little time to allow for wonder. That means we first have to stake our claim, to create a place for wonder. It's not going to happen all by itself – it involves rowing against the current for a while. But when we do stake that claim and create a fertile flowerbed, wonder will be happy to settle into that soil and grow. And in next to no time she will be rooted ever more firmly inside you.

Exercise: train your wonder muscle

Sit yourself down in a busy spot. On a beach, at a pavement café. Take a good look at the people around you, observe them. Zoom in on details, see how they interact with each other. Try not to label, just observe and remain curious. If you notice judgements bubbling up inside you ('What an idiotic jacket!' or 'Look at her, flapping about like a chicken in distress!'), see if you can shift your mood a little closer to wonder. Ask yourself questions. What is it about that jacket? What characteristics does it have? What effect is that girl's body language having on the person she's talking to? What might those gestures say about her? You will probably find yourself taking a lingering, more intense look and paying greater attention to detail. And maybe you'll start enjoying yourself that little bit more.

Advanced wonder-muscle workout

Once you feel confident enough to flex your wonder muscle a little more, you can set yourself a bigger challenge. Move on from non-committal observation to a situation in which you feel more invested. One that bothers you. Winds you up. I'm sure you know someone who always seems to get on your nerves. Someone who triggers a particular response. Before you've exchanged two words you find yourself thinking, 'Typical, here we go again!'

But this time try to push your annoyance to one side and enter into a new interaction with a sense of wonder. See this person as a companion. Instead of thinking, 'Here we go again!' or 'What a crass remark!' try to stick with your new perspective. I wonder why they said that? What's going through their head at this very moment? What are they getting out of this interaction? These are just some of the questions that might spring to mind. The key is to really feel that sense of wonder and be sincere in your questions. If you're not, the process can descend into an elaborate exercise in sarcasm, and that will be no good to you at all.

CURIOSITY: *REALLY* WANTING TO KNOW

If you want to have a satisfying conversation, one thing matters above all else: you have to be interested in what the other person has to say. And curious about what they think, their experiences, how they perceive the world. Yet often that's something we lack, and we enter into a dialogue that is secretly more interested in ourselves.

After taking a course in 'Critical Thinking' a few years ago, I was eager to tell a colleague all about the experience. My teacher had opted for an unconventional approach, one I was enthusiastic about, so I painted a verbal picture of the class, the methods he had used and the exercises we had done. It wasn't long before my colleague voiced an opinion. 'What does he think he's playing at?' he said. 'As a teacher, he's supposed to give people a safe space. What he's doing is downright irresponsible!'

I caught myself firing off one 'yes ... but' after the other, determined to defend my position and convince my colleague otherwise. 'Yes, I can see what you're getting at, but at the time it didn't feel intimidating at all. Within his method it really made sense and ...'

As I drove home, I realised what had happened. Neither of us had held back our judgement. In fact we had waded right in, without being fully informed. My colleague with his judgement of the course and the teacher I had described, and me with my judgement that my colleague's response was unjustified and over-the-top. It soon became clear what was missing: a genuine curiosity about each other's views. And the genuine questions it could have generated.

We had both been clinging to our own agendas. I had wanted to convince my colleague how inspiring this teacher and his method were, while he was determined that I should understand why the teacher had failed to respect the integrity of his students. Neither of us was interested in gaining a better understanding of the other person's view – only in finding better ways to express our own.

My colleague could have been more curious about the method and how I had experienced it. 'So why exactly did this teacher opt for those particular interventions?' 'What effect did it have on the students?' As for me, I could have been curious about why my colleague had voiced such a strong opinion. 'What exactly is it about this method that you object to?' 'Why do you think it's wrong?' 'Is it always the teacher's responsibility to make everyone feel safe, or should the students take some of that responsibility themselves?' I am sure we would have had a more fulfilling conversation if either one of us had thought to take a step back. But once you have waded into the swamp of attack and defence, of judgement and condemnation, it can be hard to find your way back.

You begin to develop a questioning attitude by learning to steer yourself from judgement towards curiosity. Towards a genuine interest in the other person's thought processes and experience. In the heat of the moment, things can move very quickly. It's only afterwards that you start to realise: I should have reacted this way or that, or I could have asked such-and-such a question. Moments of hindsight are important: the next time I have a similar conversation with someone, those moments will make me more alert and help me steer us clear of another judgemental face-off. There's no guarantee that I'll succeed in this, of course, but thinking things through and developing the intention is a valuable step in the right direction.

You never know it all

Staying curious means acknowledging there are things you don't know. You simply don't know how another person experiences something, or what they are thinking and feeling. The other person is exactly that: other, not identical to you. And although you might have an annoying father-in-law, an intimidating boss or an allergy to people who are never on time, there's every chance that, when you zoom in on those experiences, your thoughts and feelings don't exactly match those of the person you are talking to. Remember, the other person is always the expert on their own experience and we are often far too quick to assume that we know exactly what they mean.

I once gave a training course in conversation skills and questioning techniques to a group of young accountants. Their assignment was to split into pairs: one had to describe a situation in which they had felt irritated, and the other had to get to the bottom of things. I stood listening to one of the pairs for a while. Bart had just come back from a holiday and his story was set at the airport. 'We were ready for departure at 2 p.m., right on schedule. Everyone was on board, baggage stowed, seatbelts fastened. And then … nothing! No roaring engines, no taxiing to the runway. We just sat there. Forty-five minutes went by before we finally took off.'

James nodded, listened, hummed a little and said, 'Yeah, that must have been really annoying.' Then he tried to come up with a question. And couldn't. I asked him why.

'Well, as stories go, this one's pretty cut-and-dried. It all makes perfect sense to me.'

'Do you know everything about Bart's experience?' I asked.

'Well, it's obvious, isn't it? He was stuck on the plane waiting. That must have been very annoying.'

'Do you know why he found it annoying?' I asked.

'Uh … Well … it was a complete waste of time.'

'So for you, the irritation factor would be time. You think the waste of time was annoying. But who knows? Bart might have a completely different reason. Perhaps the time wasted wasn't that big a deal for him. Maybe he was anxious about take-off. Maybe he was hungry and looking forward to the in-flight meal. You don't really know for sure.'

When James then asked Bart what had been so irritating about the delay, Bart replied, 'Oh, you know what it's like, being stuck in those seats on the plane. After a while your whole body starts to seize up. I mean, it's so uncomfortable. Why didn't they let us wait in the departure lounge? At least then we'd have had some leg space!'

Trivial though this example may seem, it's a very precise illustration of what often happens in conversations: you think you have understood the other person's story; perhaps it chimes with something you experienced yourself and, acting on the notion that it's as clear as can be, you don't think to ask any further. As soon as you operate on that basis, your interest in the other person and their story begins to wane. But when you get beyond the anecdote and tap into a real curiosity about the other person's story – about their experiences, thoughts, feelings and judgements – sometimes you discover information you couldn't have imagined was there.

James saw 'time' as the overriding concept in the situation Bart described. Yet time didn't even feature in Bart's account of his own experience, which centred on the notion of 'comfort'. Following through with a question, and being interested in what's going on in the other person's mind, brings you closer to each other. As you might imagine, this will add all kinds of depth to your conversations. Constantly realising that you actually know nothing about the other person's thoughts and experiences, and at the same time being curious about them, helps you ask better questions that dig a little deeper.

An exercise in curiosity: you're the novice, they're the expert

Children are naturals at this. Animals too. So why do we adults so often get it wrong? It's because we like to think we know the score, when often we don't have the slightest idea. The next exercise is a way of getting to grips with this shortcoming.

Talk to somebody from the following perspective: I haven't a clue about this and you know it all. Think of the other person as an expert on the topic under discussion. Consider your own thoughts, judgements and opinions to be anything but interesting. What *you* think about the subject, and what you *think* you know, simply don't matter. Focus on the other person. What do they think? What were their exact experiences? Can they provide more examples? Is it always the way they described? Might it be different? If so, how? And in what circumstances?

If you do this often enough, you will notice that you never run out of questions. And if you feel like your supply of questions is starting to run dry, it's probably because you have slipped back into 'knowing' or 'agreeing' without checking the basis for your response.

COURAGE

Questions that dive beneath the surface and occasionally confront hidden truths are not the easiest things to accept. They have the potential to challenge, surprise and knock a person off-balance. As a result, the person on the receiving end sometimes has to dig deep and can even end up being surprised by their own answer. Asking questions and making room for their answers calls for courage and vulnerability. You never know in advance if your question will hit the mark or how it will be received. It means abandoning a significant degree of control and letting things happen. Your question might be uncomfortable or confrontational. You don't know if the other person will be inclined to answer or will simply be left feeling awkward, annoyed or embarrassed. Sometimes it can feel as if you've just run into a conversational brick wall.

As we have already discovered, we hold back on asking many a question for fear of unsettling the recipient. That's a real pity. How many wonderful conversations have you missed out on just because you didn't dare ask that one question?

My friend Nina knows exactly what I'm talking about. 'I'm married and my husband and I are getting to that age when people often assume we have children. When we meet new people, we regularly get asked whether we do, and when we say no, I often see the other person swallow and get a little flustered. You can almost see them thinking "I'd like to ask more, but I don't dare." On the few occasions when someone *has* asked, it's led to the most rewarding conversations. It's such a pity that we so often stop short of asking the questions we'd really like to ask.'

There are of course many different reasons why a couple might not have children – but often people prefer to make their own assumptions or change the subject rather than risk entering into what they fear might be a potentially difficult discussion. In doing so, they avoid a difficult discussion but, at the same time, also rob themselves of a potentially interesting conversation.

A good question about a potentially delicate subject often has the power to forge a connection. In Nina's case, it was daring to ask more about her life with her husband and their not having children. It's only logical that you wouldn't want to just come out with a blunt question on any old topic, however personal. But if we want better, more meaningful, truthful conversations, we will have to go a little less easy on ourselves. If the situation feels right, and the other person is up for answering the question fully, you can lay the groundwork for a frank and fascinating exchange.

We need to face up to vulnerability and discomfort and still ask that delicate question. At times you may still hit that dreaded brick wall now and again. Welcome to the club! But you'd be surprised how often a delicate and well-considered question like that strikes the recipient as appealing and engaging, as an invitation to open up. Even a question that confronts the other person with something uncomfortable can bring about a positive and liberating experience.

Building courage and a willingness to accept the risk of feeling uncomfortable is part of developing your Socratic attitude.

A weird presentation: daring to ask

Leadership coach Monique Linders told me what happened the day she turned up for a seminar entitled 'New Leadership'. A PowerPoint presentation sprang into life in a small, darkened room. Slide after slide of graphs and financial figures. Within seconds she was completely lost. What did any of this have to do with a new approach to management? She looked around for signs of confusion on the faces of the other participants. Nothing.

A good fifteen minutes in, she finally plucked up the courage to raise her hand and ask if she was at the right seminar. 'My heart was racing like mad,' she told me. 'I was so afraid of looking like an idiot for not being smart enough to link the presentation with New Leadership. The speaker began leafing nervously through his papers. After a while he bashfully had to admit that he had launched into the wrong presentation. The rest of the participants heaved a collective sigh of relief and one of them burst out, "All this time I was sat here thinking: what a weird presentation!'"

Asking a good question can feel like jumping out of a plane. You don't know for sure whether your parachute will open. You have no idea whether the landing will be soft or bumpy, or whether you'll be welcomed by the ground below. But you don't ask a good question for your own sake, or to earn yourself a happy landing. You ask a good question for the other person, so that they can think more deeply about their ideas and opinions and perhaps move on to see things in a new light. This gift to the other person can occasionally mean an awkward tumble for you. But believe me, it's a price worth paying.

Exercise: exploring your own hesitation

Have a good think about that one question you have always wanted to ask. Who would you like to put it to? What exactly is that question? What's stopping you? Is it fear of awkwardness? Your own insecurity? Are you 100 per cent sure that your question will not be well received? Think what positives asking it might bring. After all, you're curious about it for a reason.

Exercise: asking despite the awkwardness

You're going to go ahead and do it: ask that one tricky, delicate, awkward question. If you catch yourself in a conversation thinking, 'I'd really like to ask this question now, but I don't think I will', take the plunge! Ask it anyway. Your decision to ask is independent of the other person's freedom to answer or not answer. That's the next step, and that step is up to them. But you can at least resolve to take the first step towards vulnerability and a deeper connection.

You don't have to simply lob your question over the net. You can introduce it gently. For example, you might say, 'There's something I'd really like to ask, but I'm not sure whether I should. It might be a sensitive subject.' See how the other person reacts. Or you might even ask their permission beforehand: 'I'd like to ask you a question about this. Do you mind if I just put it out there? It's entirely up to you whether you want to answer it or not. Are you okay with that?'

JUDGING WITHOUT TAKING IT SERIOUSLY

We make judgements all day long, and that's just as well. Without judgement, how would you know whether you were in the mood for peanut butter or jam (or both!) on your sandwich? Whether to buy the snazzy red jacket or the slinky blue one? To say nothing of life's more monumental decisions, like which career you should pursue or which school is the best fit for your child. Judgements colour and impact every aspect of our lives, in ways both big and small:

Cauliflower or broccoli for dinner tonight?

Should I go into business with this person or that person?

Should I take this job offer or hold out for a better opportunity?

Is this guy worth a second date or should we leave it at this?

Do I intervene or let things take their course? Go on or stop?

Am I the person I want to be or is it time to start making some changes?

What kind of conduct do I disapprove of or admire? Label as good or bad?

You judge, and those judgements shape your life. It's impossible for them not to. When you meet someone for the first time, your judgement kicks in within around eight seconds and your first impression is formed: 'I like this person and feel comfortable with them' or 'No, this person's not for me.' Judging is as fundamentally human as breathing. Pretending not to judge is like a fish pretending not to swim: 'Nah, you've got it all wrong. This isn't swimming, it's … uh … flying. Yeah, that's it! I'm flying, only in water.'

Judging can make life fun, exciting, rich and manageable. Trying to shut down your sense of judgement or censor it can only lead to more misery. You catch yourself being judgemental and don't think that you should be, but giving yourself a hard time about judging simply succeeds in piling on another layer of judgement, while making yourself feel guilty and unhappy in the process. Allow yourself to judge. It will happen whether you like it or not. Judging is as human as eating, drinking, talking, breaking wind or tripping over a loose paving stone. Acting as if we don't, or shouldn't, judge anything is an odd and unhelpful thing to do. It means denying part of your humanity.

As you might expect, there is a big 'but' to all this: we tend to be very clumsy and slapdash with those judgements of ours. We are often too quick to judge, overlooking all kinds of nuances and subtleties and basing our opinions on incomplete information. We're also far too attached to what we think: we take our judgements way too seriously. Once you've decided that a person is an arrogant egotist, it can be very hard to convince yourself of anything else. It's what psychologists call 'confirmation bias': we are so eager to reinforce the judgement we've already formed that we lapse into a kind of tunnel vision and are only too happy to ignore any evidence that presents itself to the contrary.

For those who insist that judging simply isn't okay, it's worth considering that 'You're not allowed to judge' is a formidable judgement in its own right. A perfect contradiction. Statements like these usually come in response to negative judgements. I've yet to hear someone complain about being judged and being deemed talented, charming or beautiful. If Roger says, 'Fred's been so lazy and sloppy lately', we're likely to say, 'You mustn't judge him like that, Roger! Maybe he's got things on his mind!' If, on the other hand, Roger had said, 'Fred's been so dynamic and conscientious lately', no one would raise the slightest objection.

When you look at this logically, it seems a little odd: why should we be allowed to say that someone is talented, charming or gorgeous, but not lazy, arrogant, deceitful or a bit of a know-it-all? In essence, they are all examples of judgement. It looks like a case of double standards, in which judgements appear to be fine as long as they're positive ones, whereas their negative counterparts are out of order.

Perhaps it's because we often confuse condemnation and judgement. Condemnation is about disapproval and rejection, whereas to judge is to reach a conclusion by reasoning. So in Roger's case, it's possible to state rationally, clearly and demonstrably why Fred is sloppy: he never tidies his desk, his keyboard is covered in coffee stains, he doesn't keep his appointments, he rarely hits a deadline. That's a judgement: 'Fred's sloppy because …' But if you go on to conclude that being sloppy makes you a worthless human being, you have strayed into condemnation.

In so many instances, we do both things at once. We say, 'Goodness, Fred's been so sloppy!' while our expression and intonation betray exactly what we think of that observation. We judge and condemn at one and the same time.

Developing a Socratic attitude is about separating the two: seeing a situation for what it is and judging it as objectively as possible. And the next step is to question that judgement by asking, 'Is that really the case? Is what I'm saying or thinking here actually true?'

I applaud the fact that we judge. But I also advocate everyone taking more responsibility for their judgements and handling them with greater care. Making those judgements as objectively as possible and developing a readiness to renounce them immediately, if need be. This is the essence of the agile perspective we are looking to find: you judge and then you adopt a position, but you don't cling to that position and enmesh your own identity with it. This approach means you are free to explore the opposite view just as readily. You see your judgement for what it is: *your* individual view of reality. You realise that you can, and should, examine that view more closely, that it forms the basis for your unconscious assumptions, your presuppositions or prejudices and your view of human nature. Once you realise this and actively start trying to see things from another perspective, you'll soon see how much stronger, more flexible and agile your own thinking becomes.

Another piece of advice we're given all the time: you have to suspend judgement. I honestly don't believe that's realistic. Judgements are made quickly, unconsciously, reflexively. Before you know where you are, another one has formed.

Delaying an unconscious process is no small feat and may not be possible at all. I think the solution lies somewhere else: in making your judgement, being aware of it and then taking a step back from it. Register your own judgement, then lift it out of the conversation and let it fade into the background. You don't so much suspend your judgement as withdraw it. It's unavoidably going to be there, so take note of it and then resolve to do nothing with it.

This process lies at the heart of the Socratic attitude: knowing that you are always judging what's in front of you, while also knowing there are probably several sides to every issue. Have a judgement, step back from it and dare to explore it. Turn it upside down and inside out, bounce it off the walls and see what happens. Judge your judgement in its turn. Toss it in the bin, fish it back out, dust it off and look at it from another angle. Bin it again and repeat.

A parable: good or bad, who's to say?

Here's a wonderful story that can teach us something about judging, withdrawing our judgements and how deeply ingrained our judgements are within our being. It's a parable about a farmer and his son:

> In a village in rural China lived a farmer and his son. Besides their humble dwelling and their land, their only possession of value was a horse. Owning that horse

meant they could work the land and earn a modest living. One day the horse escaped from the paddock and ran away. The villagers came to express their sympathy. 'How awful!' they cried. 'What a disaster!' The farmer just smiled and said calmly, 'Good or bad, who's to say? All I know is that my horse ran away.'

In the days that followed, the farmer and his son went out and worked the land as best they could. One day, off in the distance, they saw a horse. It was their horse! The animal had returned, bringing with it a string of seven wild horses.

When they heard the news, the villagers were so happy for the farmer that they rushed over to congratulate him. 'Oh, what luck, what good fortune!' they cried. 'So many horses, and all of them yours!' The farmer just smiled and said calmly, 'Good or bad, who's to say? All I know is that my horse has returned, bringing seven horses with him.'

The next day the farmer's son wanted to break in one of the new horses. He jumped on its back, but the horse bucked and reared wildly and the son came crashing to the ground. The fall broke both his legs.

That evening the villagers came to see the farmer and lamented the fate of his poor son. 'What a disaster!' they cried. 'This poor young man, both legs broken. What terrible misfortune!' The farmer just smiled and said calmly, 'Good or bad, who's to say? All I know is that both my son's legs are broken.'

The next day the army arrived in the village with a proclamation. Two soldiers called at every home. War had broken out and every man who was fit enough to fight had to report for duty immediately. When they saw the state the farmer's son was in, they granted him an exemption. The farmer just smiled and said calmly …

The moral of the story of the farmer and his son can be summed up in any number of ways: wait and see how things turn out; you never know what good or bad might come of something; dark clouds can have silver linings. The farmer's refrain – 'Good or bad, who's to say?' – shows us a stoic perspective and an enlightened attitude that we often have trouble achieving.

The response of the villagers is much more familiar to us. They personify the speed at which we rush to categorise the events in our lives. Is the news good or bad? Has good fortune come or has disaster struck? Do we stand to lose or benefit? At times our readiness to pigeonhole facts, events, developments and behaviour seems to border on the obsessive. That readiness is something we need to fight against, if we ever hope to achieve wonder and curiosity and start asking deeper questions. We need to realise that in most cases we are just not well enough informed to have an immediate opinion. That we, like the farmer, should take judgement out of the equation and put it on ice for a while. We can always come back to it tomorrow and see if it's still useful. By that time our judgement may have changed. Perhaps it will have had a chance to grow or mature a little. Who knows what nugget of fresh information might have turned up in the meantime to give it new shape?

How do you judge more carefully?

Being more careful about your judgements is easier said than done. You hear or see something on the news, your colleague makes a remark, your boss asks you a question, you hear a tasty piece of gossip from a friend and, before you know it, you've slapped a sticker on it and popped it in a pigeonhole. Judgement has been passed, but the resulting opinion often says more about your own values and view of human nature than it does about the actual situation. How can you avoid judging too quickly?

One inspiring philosophy that can help you be less ready to judge is that of the Stoics. Nowadays the word 'stoic' has a bit of a grim connotation: emotionless, unmoving, unapproachable. It's a shame we think of it that way, because Stoic philosophy has so much more to offer.

The Stoics don't owe their name to anything grim at all, but to the *stoa*, a portico in ancient Athens where people often came together to philosophise. Stoic philosophy is a practical philosophy, which calls on us to focus on what we can control, and resign ourselves to matters over which we have no influence. The result is peace of mind. The Stoics developed a range of practical exercises and meditations aimed at developing a virtuous life. Stoicism went through several periods and the philosophy was influenced by a series of prominent thinkers.

One of the most important Stoic philosophers was Epictetus. In his *Enchiridion*, a short manual of ethical advice, he wrote about everyday issues, among which he included our tendency to judge. He invites his readers to simply observe, without judgement:

> If a man wash quickly, do not say that he washes badly, but that he washes quickly. If a man drink much wine, do not say that he drinks badly, but that he drinks much. For till you have decided what judgement prompts him, how do you know that he acts badly? If you do as I say, you will assent to your apprehensive impressions and to none other.[4]

In his recent book *How to Be a Stoic*, writer and philosophy professor Massimo Pigliucci takes this a step further:

> The idea is to distinguish between matters of fact – to which we can assent if we find them justified by observation – and judgements, from which we generally ought to abstain, since we usually don't have sufficient information.[5]

Exercise: register your judgement

Each new day brings countless opportunities for training yourself to be more careful about your judgements. The bus you just missed, your sarcastic colleague, a rude passer-by: all everyday occurrences that trigger a snap response. The first step is to realise that you are probably slapping a label on these things. When you find yourself in those situations, ask yourself a few simple questions. What do I think of this? How would I sum up this situation, or this person, in one or two words? Stupid, satisfying, arrogant, impatient, beautiful, ugly, too fast, too slow …

This simple exercise helps you conceptualise what you think and see, and in doing so you learn to distance yourself from your own thinking.

Another thing worth noticing is whether you condemn your own thoughts. Do you find yourself thinking 'I shouldn't think this is good!' or 'Perhaps things aren't so bad, I shouldn't be so fatalistic'?

Exercise: practising agile perspective

Once you are aware of the judgements that ambush you and are able to articulate them clearly without immediately trying to counter them or stop them in their tracks, you are ready for the next step: seeking out and practising agile perspective. The next time you find yourself in a situation that triggers a strong urge to judge, take some time for the next exercise:

1. Write your judgement down as literally as possible. What exactly were you thinking?
2. Describe the situation that led up to your judgement, again as literally as you can.
3. Think of three judgements someone else might make when faced with exactly the same situation.
4. Think of one argument in support of each of these judgements.
5. See how these alternative judgements could also be 'true'.

Simply going through these steps gives you some headspace, creates room to breathe and opens up different perspectives. Here's an example:

Thought:	There goes Natalie, complaining as usual.
Situation:	Natalie was talking to Jonathan at the coffee machine. She said, 'Oh God, I'm so busy! I just don't have the time to finish this job. I had to work late yesterday and couldn't pick up my daughter from school. It really got me down!' As she spoke she frowned and sighed.

Alternative judgements someone might make in the same situation:	1. Natalie trusts Jonathan enough to share her story.
	2. Natalie feels the need to talk about her concerns.
	3. Natalie is having a good old moan and that's entirely up to her.

Exercise: become a Stoic – judge objectively

With Epictetus's words about washing 'quickly' and drinking 'much' at the back of your mind, you can train yourself to be a Stoic. Stick to the facts, register the judgement you are making, be aware that judgement is always a response to a factual observation and keep mindful of the difference between the two. For instance:

| Judgement: | It's about time Harry ironed his shirt. |
| Fact: | Harry's shirt looks like it hasn't been ironed. |

An interesting intermediate step is to question that judgement. In this case you might ask, 'Who thinks Harry should iron his shirt?' The answer can only be: 'Well, I do.' The next question is obvious: 'Who am I to tell Harry to iron his shirt?' Most likely you're not in a position to set standards for Harry and his laundry habits.

The difference between observing and interpreting

I mentioned earlier that, some years back, I worked as a riding instructor, when I also offered sessions that combined personal coaching with riding. Being coached while you interact with horses can provide a fascinating window into your own behaviour, your convictions and your energy. While horses can't speak to us directly, they are sensitive translators of our body language.

The sessions worked like this: I got people to work with their horse or one of my horses, gave them assignments as they rode around the pen and then we reflected on what happened. One of their first tasks was to observe. I got them to stand at the edge of the pen, look at the horse and asked them, 'What do you see?' This simplest of questions almost always elicited an answer along the lines of: 'He's curious.' 'He's afraid.' 'He's not in the mood. You can tell because he's looking away.' 'He's hungry because he's chewing on a blade of grass.'

If the person was doing the session with their own horse, their answers were often more detailed. 'She's just being stubborn now, but she often does that.' 'She's shy because you're here.' 'She can hear all kinds of new noises and it's got her on edge – look, her ears are twitching in all directions.'

It was very rare for someone to do what I had asked them to do. In other words, just tell me what they saw. Hardly anyone stuck to simple observations. 'The horse is walking to the left.' 'The horse is looking off into the distance.' 'Look, now he's munching on a tuft of grass.' Or 'His ears are pointing towards his tail.' Once I'd explained the difference between *observing* and *interpreting*, the penny often dropped. Then I'd ask them, 'Are you describing what you see objectively or are you interpreting the horse's behaviour?' Once they were in the right frame of mind to make clear observations, their interpretations also became purer. They became more like hypotheses: assumptions that had yet to be proven. After all, you can't say for sure that your mare is feeling restless, scared or angry. At most you can say that her behaviour makes you think she might be these things.

I came to realise that what I had discovered through working with horses also applies to how we see other people. With people, too, it's very difficult to stick to pure observation. Before you know it, interpretations are flitting around your brain like pigeons around Trafalgar Square. Developing a Socratic attitude means training your senses to observe objectively, without inviting your brain to weigh in and turn those observations into interpretations based on a narrative of your own creation.

Exercise: observing instead of interpreting

Try observing someone you don't know. Once again, a busy outdoor space is the place to be. Pick a pavement café or a square, where you can settle down for a while and watch from a distance without being conspicuous. Observe and literally state what you see. If you see what looks like a couple arguing – your interpretation – ease back into literal observation: the woman is gesturing with her right arm, a little crease has appeared between her eyebrows; the man looks up, sighs and yells, 'That's what I've been trying to tell you!'

It's logical to conclude that this is a couple having a row. And that conclusion might be spot on. But how many times do we draw a conclusion that's just a little off the mark? We take one look at the person we're talking to and think, 'You're a jerk' or 'Someone got out of bed the wrong side this morning.' Observing objectively helps you take some distance, and the quality of your final judgement usually improves as a result.

LEARNING TO PUT UP WITH (AND EVEN EMBRACE) NOT-KNOWING

Practising a Socratic attitude means that you question what you think you know for sure, even to the point of ultimately not being sure at all. As odd as it sounds, it helps to train your capacity for not-knowing. It's only the absence of supposed knowledge that makes space for new, genuine knowledge. Constantly testing the outer limits of your certainty gives you the opportunity to make new discoveries.

One philosopher who can teach us about radical doubt is René Descartes, a French thinker who lived between 1596 and 1650. He is best known for his statement 'I think, therefore I am.' In his search for something he could be absolutely sure of, he developed the process of methodical doubt: he systematically doubted everything he possibly could. If you dispense with everything that can be doubted, Descartes reasoned, you are left with what is necessarily true.

For Descartes, the starting point for true knowledge was to radically doubt everything we think we know. His goal was to obtain true knowledge. He settled down in front of a crackling fire – or at least that's how I like to picture him – and began a systematic search for what was true beyond any shadow of a doubt. He applied his methodology by questioning every one of his long-held convictions. And when he hit upon something he thought he was sure of, he tried to undermine it with counter-arguments.

Sitting in his chair by the fire, it can't have taken him long to hit upon the thought 'I know because my senses tell me.' But as he thought more deeply, even his senses became subject to doubt. After all, the senses telling you that you're sitting in a nice, warm chair this minute are the same senses you experience when you're dreaming. And dreams appear true to life, don't they?

Besides, you are fooled by your senses on a regular basis. How many times have you thought you heard something move behind you, only to turn round and find there's nothing there? Or felt your phone vibrate when it wasn't in your pocket? Okay, Descartes didn't come up with that last example, but he easily could have, if he were alive and making his case today. In the end, Descartes concluded that our senses are not the most reliable source of knowledge.

But gazing into the fire, he eventually arrived at one thing he couldn't possibly doubt. He was sure that he was thinking. As a result of his methodical doubt, he had begun to have misgivings about the reality of the world around him and his sensory perceptions of it – but he *knew* that he was doubting. Whichever way he looked at it, there was a 'thinking entity'. This gave rise to his famous *Cogito, ergo sum*: I think, therefore I am. As we develop a questioning Socratic attitude, we can take Descartes as an inspiration. If you look very attentively, and examine all your certainties with the aim of doubting them, you soon appreciate that, when it comes down to it, you hardly know anything for sure at all.

Exercise: doubt yourself silly!

Think of something you're completely and utterly certain of. Which of your convictions would you class as an absolute truth? Write that conviction down. Then ask yourself, 'Is this absolutely true?' Start by answering that question positively – 'Yes, this is absolutely true because …' – and write down every argument you can think of for holding that conviction.

What proof do you have? (In case you were wondering, 'That's just the way it is' or 'That's how I feel about things' doesn't count!) Then try to write down the most compelling arguments *against* your conviction. Ask yourself the same question, but this time begin your answer with 'No, this isn't true because ...' What might someone who disagrees with you say about the matter? And at what point do you find yourself agreeing with them?

Take another look at your original statement. You may well find that this exercise has created a little more room for movement and for doubt, and that your conviction has loosened up a little: something no longer set in stone and that you can wear more lightly. Does that level of flexibility seem like a scary prospect? That's a valid response, and useful information in its own right: it gives you an idea of how attached you are to your beliefs, to 'knowing something for sure'.

Wu Wei and not-knowing

The Taoists have a concept they call Wu Wei. Roughly translated, Wu Wei is the art of not-doing. Many people confuse not-doing with simply doing nothing. Plain old passivity, in other words. But that's missing the point. As Tao trainer Reinoud Eleveld explains,[6] practising Wu Wei does not equate to doing nothing. There's no real art in doing nothing: you avoid action and nothing happens. Whereas

Wu Wei – the art of not-doing – is just as likely to lead to action as inaction.

At its core, Wu Wei is about the ability to act without the interference of ego or, to put it another way, our conscious sense of ourselves. It is a pure action, born of natural instinct, excellence and wisdom. It is called the art of not-doing because at crucial moments the ego is bypassed and does nothing. It might observe, but it does not take control of the individual's response.

Eleveld likes to illustrate this elusive concept using the example of the 'bystander effect'. Imagine that an elderly man falls into a canal in a busy urban district. To do nothing at that moment is to stand there watching a man in trouble, someone in serious danger of drowning. Everyone stands there waiting for somebody else to intervene. Meanwhile the person in distress drowns, with dozens of people looking on. That is the bystander effect in action: disaster strikes and, although there are plenty of people around, nobody does a thing.

The bystander effect can be extrapolated to all kinds of threats facing our society. We'd like to see an end to racism and bigotry, but what are we doing to combat it? We'd like fewer young people to fall prey to sex trafficking, but what are we doing to keep them safe? We'd like to see the end to global warming and the use of fossil fuels, but many of us would rather keep driving our beaten-up old car than go electric.

But back to the canal. A person who is in touch with Wu Wei – the art of not-doing – will not simply stand by and do nothing when they see the elderly man in distress. A practitioner of Wu Wei will jump into the water without hesitation, without worrying about ruining their shoes or clothing, or about how many people might be watching. Far from being passive, someone in touch with Wu Wei will act decisively and without a trace of misgiving. They will intervene without a thought for their self-interest and do everything they can to help the elderly man reach safety.

In exploring concepts such as doubt, there are things to be learned from Wu Wei and the art of not-doing. Just as doing nothing is different from the Wu Wei principle of not-doing, so having doubt is also not the same thing as not-knowing.

At first glance, doubt and not-knowing might seem to resemble each other. They both imply an absence of knowledge, but the difference lies in the fact that doubt brings uncertainty, while not-knowing is a more robust, more conscious experience. When it comes to developing a questioning and Socratic attitude, the concept of not-knowing is much more useful to us.

Doubt and not-knowing are still related, of course. I sometimes like to think of doubt as not-knowing's neurotic sibling. Just as Wu Wei, a pure form of action, arises from tranquillity and has nothing to do with ego, not-knowing is also born from that same pure and tranquil state of mind. When you are in doubt, you are tangled up in the object of your doubts; not-knowing takes a step back and maintains distance:

- Not-knowing observes without wanting anything; doubt watches and hopes for a resolution.
- Not-knowing is about consciously abandoning certainty; doubt is about looking for certainty.
- Not-knowing is an open palm; doubt grasps and clings.
- Not-knowing gazes calmly; the eyes of doubt dart back and forth.
- Not-knowing stands still and experiences; doubt shifts and searches.
- Not-knowing has a wide field of vision; doubt has a narrow focus.
- Not-knowing is patient; doubt demands answers.
- Not-knowing is connected with itself; doubt reaches for something outside itself.
- Not-knowing does not want to solve anything and accepts itself; doubt wants to resolve itself and above all not to exist.
- Not-knowing is rooted in tranquillity and trust; doubt is born of fear.
- Not-knowing offers you a warm home, while in the house that doubt built, the heating is always on the blink.

Suppose you're in a meeting. A meeting where thorny issues have to be addressed and decisions have to be made. Needless to say, you have a hundred other things on the go, churning away at the back of your mind. The meeting has come at the worst possible time and will probably drag on for ever. But there's nothing else for it: those decisions have to be taken now, arguments have to be laid on the table and options have to be discussed.

But before you plunge headlong into that process, what if you said to each other, 'Let's just take five minutes to not-know'? What effect might that have?

Perhaps it would lead to a situation in which everyone sat and thought for a bit, and maybe scribbled the odd idea or thought on a piece of paper as they weighed up the pros and cons in their own minds. Perhaps a position already taken might be re-examined, or even confirmed, but this time with arguments that were more considered. Five minutes without being bombarded with another person's outspoken opinion. Alone with your own thought processes and your own not-knowing.

Very often we just say whatever comes into our heads. Sure, it's an opinion and you're prepared to defend it, but later, when the moment has passed, we can often end up disagreeing with ourselves.

SHELVING YOUR EMPATHY

When you want to ask tightly focused, well-observed questions that get you or someone else thinking, oddly enough empathy won't get you very far. If your aim is to ask a good question, it's better to have your empathic powers switched off rather than on. In many schools of thought and coaching settings, dialling down empathy is considered the crime of the century. Where would we be without empathy? It's our passport to a better world! But before you think this book heartless, slam it shut and chuck it into the corner in a fit of rage, give me the benefit of the doubt for a moment. See it as an opportunity to practise those newly acquired skills of wonder and curiosity.

Let's start at the beginning: what is empathy? What is it good for? Empathy is a word that gets bandied about and used in any number of ways, but mostly it boils down to the ability to understand someone else's situation and appreciate how they feel. To experience the world as they experience it, or at least how you *imagine* they might experience it. Empathy means putting yourself in the other person's shoes. At first sight, you might ask yourself: what could possibly be wrong with that? Surely empathy can only help me understand them better? Yes, of course it can, and it should come as no surprise that empathy has a broad and enthusiastic fan base. But empathy can also be your greatest enemy if you are trying to make well-considered ethical choices, ask in-depth questions and cultivate that all-important agile perspective.

Paul Bloom, a psychologist at Yale University, wrote a book with the telling title *Against Empathy*. In an article for the *Boston Review*, he writes:

> When asked what I am working on, I often say I am writing a book about empathy. People tend to smile and nod, and then I add, 'I'm against it.' This usually gets an uncomfortable laugh.
>
> This reaction surprised me at first, but I've come to realise that taking a position against empathy is like announcing that you hate kittens – a statement so outlandish it can only be a joke.[7]

Bloom goes on to explain that he is not against morality, compassion, being a good neighbour, doing the right thing or making the world a better place. In fact he is a fervent advocate of all these things. It's just that he advises against empathy as a way to achieve them. In Bloom's opinion, if you want to be a good person and want to do good, empathy is often a poor counsellor.

He admits that, in theory, empathy is a force for helping others and doing good in the world, but understands that's not exactly how it works in practice. Research shows that our feelings of empathy tend to have a certain bias: towards people in our own social group, people who look like we do, people who are very good-looking or young children. In other words, our empathy is anything but inclusive.

Bloom makes a distinction between cognitive and emotional empathy. Cognitive empathy means using your powers of reasoning to put yourself in another person's mental state, which can be very useful. He gives the example of a doctor who has to give a negative diagnosis: it helps, of course, if they are able to gauge the impact this bad news will have on the patient. That is a reasoned estimation, a wise use of social intelligence. But emotional empathy is another story. Should medical professionals also immerse themselves in the patient's feelings? Bloom's answer is no: as a consequence of emotional empathy, a surgeon could become so upset that they are left unable to operate. In other scenarios where it is appropriate to maintain a certain distance – such as making a moral judgement – our direct emotions are not much good to us. Moral judgements benefit not from empathy but from rational reflection.

In his book and his articles, Bloom argues for an alternative to emotional empathy: a quality that he calls 'non-empathetic compassion'. In the long run, he says, it's far more beneficial. The problem with emotional empathy – feeling the other person's pain – is that it greatly affects your ability to judge objectively.

Imagine your best friend's partner has died. A truly empathic reaction would be to feel their pain right along with them. To mirror their panic and their sadness as effectively as you can. However, it's worth asking whether that's likely to do your friend any good – to say nothing of yourself. A compassionate response is more likely to benefit everyone concerned, enabling you to offer help and support without being overcome by your best friend's grief.

In situations where maintaining some degree of distance is appropriate, it's *compassion*, not empathy, that you need. Compassion creates a desire to help and, unlike empathy, creates a small measure of distance, allowing you to maintain an overview of events, avoid getting too caught up in your emotions and be better at listening and analysing. It's only by shelving your empathy that you can ask worthwhile questions that dig a little deeper, that are about the other person and not about you, and that reveal more detail, expose concepts and offer confrontation where necessary. You keep empathy off-limits for a while precisely because the other person and their story matter so much to you.

In Socratic discussion this is known as 'empathic neutrality'. You switch off your tendency to share in the feelings and suffering of others in order to maintain a certain distance and retain the ability to ask critical questions. Empathic neutrality is the point at which you can register emotions and their expressions without confirming or denying them. When, during a conversation, your empathic response kicks in and compels you to offer help, give a tip or share an experience of your own, the flow of thinking trickles to a halt.

If you manage to stay empathically neutral, you create the space for someone to stick with their own thought processes and dig a little deeper. In certain situations it is the greatest gift you can give someone.

Empathic neutrality allows you to persist in your questioning. You take a step back from both the person you are talking to and the subject of the conversation, so that you can see which question will challenge the other person, deepen their insight and help their thinking. Of course, this goes hand-in-hand with pure and attentive listening, something we'll look at in more detail later.

Empathic neutrality in Socratic discussion

Socrates was a master at deactivating his powers of empathy. In his conversations he was relentless in his questioning of facts, arguments and assumptions. His commitment to empathic neutrality often made others uneasy or moved them to anger or shame. They had thought they might be lulled into a false sense of security with a sympathetic 'I know what you mean' or 'Goodness, what a pity.' But it was precisely because he refused to empathise that a conversation with Socrates was one worth having. People really gave their position some thought. Concepts took on a different, deeper meaning and there was room for new insights. If Socrates had responded empathically – 'Oh, I can see you're upset, I feel really bad for you. Let's go for a beer instead' – we would have missed out on the wealth of understanding that his dialogues have to offer.

Yet in our everyday lives we so often take a different path. Spurred on by the self-imposed assignment to be empathic, we do our very best to feel the other person's pain at the expense of asking some very necessary and relevant questions. There are times when the person you're talking to will benefit so much more from a well-chosen question than from a well-meant empathic pat on the shoulder.

Are you starting to see the downside of empathy? And what empathic neutrality can do for you?

Empathic neutrality in practice: Henriette's philosophical exploration

I run a philosophical practice where people can come for help in exploring a life question that's really important to them. Usually one that's been on their mind for a while – one they haven't managed to answer to their own satisfaction, despite thinking about it long and hard. We look at the question together, along with all the other questions and presuppositions that underlie it.

You could say that my role is to badger my questioning client with even more ruthless questions. Questions that stimulate, that make them think and can even have the power to unsettle. The goal is never to push someone beyond their limits or to rub their nose in their own contradictions.

Instead, the goal is to become wiser together – wiser about what they are actually thinking and the basis for that thinking. In an empathically neutral frame of mind, we come together to examine the issue as a whole. 'Does what you are thinking really make sense?' 'Is it logical?' We unravel the big ball of thoughts in which they have become entangled. We pick apart the ways in which one thought leads to another, look at the presuppositions behind statements, and question judgements and assumptions.

Analysing who you are and what you think is exactly what needs to happen in such a conversation. As Socrates said, 'Know thyself.' That also means acknowledging the unpleasant, less attractive, shameful parts of yourself; looking in a mirror in the clearest light possible and being brutally honest about who you are and what you think.

To know thyself means to discover that sometimes you are selfish, rude or an arsehole, that you sometimes discriminate or act unreasonably and behave in ways that are petty and manipulative. These are labels that we are so quick to slap on someone else, but seldom want to apply to ourselves. Only once you take a radically honest look at yourself can you really get to grips with knowing your whole self, warts and all.

Henriette came to see me for a philosophical consultation. She had a problem she couldn't quite get to grips with. Approaching sixty, she taught ethics and religious studies at a secondary school. Her initial question was: am I racist? An uncommon question about a sensitive issue. It takes courage to ask yourself a question like that, and even more courage to explore it with someone else in a philosophical dialogue. She knew that she was embarking on a ruthless search for truth: you don't enter the philosophical arena in search of empathy. She was going to be confronted with her innermost thoughts and asked to substantiate them. The answer could well end up being 'Yes, I am a racist.' To honestly face up to a truth like that can open the door to all kinds of pain and discomfort.

Henriette was determined to explore this idea about herself, but there was nothing light-hearted or easy about her quest: it was mired in self-censorship. Many of the biggest questions in our lives are beset with shame and guilt: that's why it's so tempting to sidestep them and distract ourselves with a glass of wine, an evening of Netflix or mindlessly scrolling Facebook. But Henriette had plucked up the courage to ask herself this question, with me as her companion and her guide.

I asked her to specify the thoughts that she had labelled as racist. Her reaction was one of pure shame. 'No, I just can't say the words. I'm afraid to. I teach ethics and religion, for goodness' sake! I'm supposed to set an example and it's just wrong for me to be thinking such things.' We began by talking about her job, and her answers revealed a set of strongly held values that 'Someone who teaches ethics and religious studies should behave in a certain way and should not entertain the wrong kinds of thoughts.' She soon came to accept that a conviction like that doesn't hold up unless you believe yourself to be some kind of perfect, moral superhero.

After a little while of talking things through, she finally worked up the courage to say her racist thought out loud: 'I sometimes think black people are less intelligent than white people.' As soon as she said the words, she turned bright red and stammered an apology. 'I'm so sorry. But that's what I mean. It doesn't make any sense. I'm just not allowed to think like that.'

This is where empathic neutrality comes in. If I had reacted empathically, I would have tried to make her feel better. But that would have been no help to her at all.

Most of the time we are happy to plaster over these unpleasant thoughts and truths about ourselves with stop-gaps like 'I'm probably no worse than anyone else' or 'Everyone has certain thoughts now and again that they don't admit to.' But a philosophical dialogue is not in the business of soothing or covering up: it exists to help you track down your unconscious thoughts, judgements, assumptions and presumptions. With the aim of subjecting them to a series of searching and critical questions.

A thought that has nestled in your head and influences the way you look at the world has no business being smoothed over, trivialised, condemned or tucked up and put to bed under a cute little heart-covered blanket. A thought like Henriette's is worth examining sincerely and should be tested by asking the question 'Is what I'm thinking here *true*?' Only then can you look at it clearly and critically, and decide afresh whether it corresponds to your view of the world and human nature.

So instead of trying to empathise with her, I asked Henriette what evidence she had that made her think black people were less intelligent than white people. 'Well,' she said, 'when I look around me, in the school staffroom, for example, or at an academic conference, I always see far more white people than black people. White people are always better represented there, so they must be better educated than black people. That's what my conclusion is based on.'

Her reasoning here belongs to the category 'anecdotal arguments': taking one situation from your personal experience and using it to draw a general conclusion. Along the lines of 'My granny smoked, too, and she lived to be ninety-three, so smoking can't be *that* bad for you.' It's easier for an outsider to debunk such a claim. There's no logic in applying the case of one grandmother to smoking in general, yet we do this kind of thing all the time. And more to the point, when we say these things we genuinely believe them.

If someone is 'stuck' in their thinking like this, your goal as a questioner is to get their critical faculties ticking over again. You're looking for something that can bring about a change of perspective, a way to see things differently, to shine a new light on that previous assertion. And for that you need distance. Overview. A clear and uncluttered mind. What you don't need is empathy.

In Henriette's case, I opted for a 'what if' question: 'What if next month you were sent to a secondary school in Nigeria on an exchange project. Imagine looking around the staffroom. What would that be like?' Henriette was quiet for a moment, thinking. 'Different,' she said. 'Of course there will be more black people teaching there.'

'So?' I asked. Sometimes a single word backed up by a question mark is enough to nudge someone towards forming a sounder conclusion.

'So I can conclude that the demographic circles I move in are limited. And that my assumption about black people isn't true and says more about my own situation and the people around me. What I thought of as logical evidence isn't really logical at all.'

'Do you have any more evidence to support your idea that black people are less intelligent than white people?' I asked. Sometimes you have to work through several arguments to get to the bottom line. She thought long and hard. 'No. This is the only one.' I pursued a few more avenues of enquiry, checking there really weren't any other thoughts that might serve as evidence for her initial conclusion. She didn't find any, no matter how hard we looked.

Henriette's thought simply didn't hold up under scrutiny. She had built a judgement on an observation that was more or less confined to her own staffroom. On this basis, she had drawn a conclusion that she had not thought to question for some time. Over time it had become something she assumed to be true until, eventually, she started to reflect on this thought, only to be alarmed by it. Once we had unravelled this process in our conversation, she was briefly confused and then a wave of relief washed over her and a new realisation dawned: it became clear to her how she had built this damaged mental structure. Not only was she able to identify the parts that were rotten and in need of replacement, but she also had the mental freedom and flexibility to check and explore other aspects of her thinking.

The consultation with Henriette is an illustration of how someone can become so caught up in their own thinking that there seems to be no way out. They end up going round in circles. This kind of thinking is often accompanied by a running commentary: you have a thought, but decide it's a bad thought that you shouldn't be having and so you can't bring yourself to examine it properly. But when you do have the courage to question it, it gives you room to think. You create new options for yourself. There's no point talking to someone who comforts and reassures you on the basis of empathy, or who slaps you down by saying, 'That's no way to think!' You need someone who genuinely takes in what you're saying, but who also allows for a bit of distance and dares to ask questions which go that little bit further.

Exercise: train your empathic neutrality

Resolve to have a conversation in which all you do is ask questions. This exercise works best if you can find a buddy and explain what you want to practise. Ask the other person to talk about something that has irritated them, something still fresh in their mind from the past few weeks. The guy who jumped the queue at the supermarket, the tailgater on the motorway, the blazing row with their in-laws, an incident at work.

While the other person talks, you listen. Don't identify with their plight or confirm their emotions. Steer well clear of remarks like 'How rude!' or 'That's a shame!' Just listen and keep quiet. Then, when the other person has finished speaking, ask a single factual question. Who else was there? How long did the row go on for? How did you feel? What made you angry? Once you have asked your question, keep quiet again and listen. Then, when the other person has answered, ask another question. Repeat this process. It's bound to feel counter-intuitive. We're all so used to chatting along and offering the other person confirmation as they talk. But that's how it should feel: empathic neutrality is the radical opposite of our comfortable conversational habits.

Develop your Socratic response

A film I never tire of watching is *12 Angry Men*, a classic courtroom drama. It centres on twelve jurors, all of them male – such was life in 1957 – who have to decide the fate of a teenager from the wrong side of the tracks who stands accused of killing his father.

These 'twelve men and true' are told that if they pronounce a guilty verdict, the boy will be sentenced to death. Not only that, but their verdict, whether 'guilty' or 'innocent', must be unanimous. After the courtroom presentations the twelve retire to the jury room and begin their deliberations.

They decide to take a first vote. The chairman asks those who think the boy is guilty to raise their hand. At this point we are fifteen minutes into the film. The twelve men, each with their own character, inclinations and frustrations, cast their vote. Eleven raise their hand and start looking around in exasperation for the sole dissenter: juror number eight, played by Henry Fonda. What follows is a fascinating analysis of group dynamics.

One juror starts chuckling, 'Boy-oh-boy! There's always one.'

'You really think he's innocent?' another juror asks.

'I don't know,' Fonda answers after a moment's hesitation.

'I mean, you sat in court and heard the same things we did. The man's a dangerous killer. You could see it.'

'Eleven men here agree,' someone else adds. 'Nobody had to think twice about it, except you.'

'I want to ask you something,' says another. 'Do you believe his story?'

Fonda replies, 'I don't know whether I believe it or not. Maybe I don't … It's just that we're talking about somebody's life here. I mean, we can't decide in five minutes. Suppose we're wrong.'[8]

The response of the other jurors is a textbook example of group dynamics: the majority will always try to convince the minority. The jury chairman makes no bones about it: 'Now perhaps if the gentleman who's disagreeing down there could tell us why. You know, tell us what he thinks – we could show him where he's probably mixed up.'

His neighbour adds, 'It seems to me it's up to us to convince this gentleman that we're right and he's wrong. Maybe if we each took a minute or two …'

The overwhelming reflex in a group is to bring the minority around to the majority group position as quickly as possible. 'That one gentleman' needs convincing that the group is right. I don't know about you, but it's a reflex I certainly recognise from meetings, larger gatherings or group discussions. Even during family conversations around the kitchen table when I was young, the dissenting voice always had to be brought into line, steered back towards the group consensus and the sooner the better.

The Socratic response is the radical opposite of this: it's about giving the voice of the minority all the space it needs. Why? Because that's where interesting points of view, new ideas, alternative options and a fresh outlook are to be found. We are often far too quick to silence other voices, even though there is great wisdom to be found there.

In *12 Angry Men* Henry Fonda finally manages to convince each of the other eleven jurors of the defendant's innocence. By reviewing all the evidence thoroughly and critically, more and more jurors are persuaded to change their mind. In the end, the boy is acquitted.

Exercise: train your Socratic response

When you meet someone with a dissenting opinion, an argument that rubs you up the wrong way, or even a point of view you find reprehensible, ease back from your initial tendency to try to 'fix' the other person. Instead take some time to immerse yourself in their thinking. What's the worst that can happen? At best, it might lead to a new insight or two and, in the process, the other person's thinking might be jogged, too. Both of you could end up a little wiser.

'Kick out all the foreigners!' The Socratic response pushed to extremes

Training your Socratic reflex is one thing; keeping it in play when the going gets tough is quite another. A high-school teacher I know once told me about a student of his. Let's call him Danny. During a class discussion one day he came out with the statement 'It's time we kicked out all the foreigners!'

It's bound to be a bit of a shock when one of your students lets rip with an opinion like that. Your reflex could well be to jump in and correct them, to get them to change their views then and there. You might feel your anger rising or an urge to send them out of class or give them a disciplinary exercise as punishment.

In essence, the message flashing up inside your head is 'You shouldn't even be thinking that, never mind blurting it out in front of everyone!' That's understandable, but the chances are that response won't be particularly helpful. If you air that view, Danny will be far more likely to dig in and defend his own position than to indulge in a spot of agile perspective. Instead try to draw some inspiration from the likes of Socrates and Epictetus. If you let them guide you, you may well make some progress.

Go with your Socratic response, tap into your curiosity and wonder, and ask Danny a genuine question. In these instances, when the other person's thinking is so far removed from your own, there is a world of difference to discover and a lot of ground to cover. It doesn't matter if you completely disagree with what the other person has to say; no one *has* to end up agreeing with anyone. What you are doing is making a genuine effort to put yourself in the other person's position, without passing judgement. This last point about judgement is vital, because it's all too easy to ask a question that hints at criticism, aversion or disgust and then you simply won't get anywhere.

In Danny's case, you might ask, 'Which foreigners do you mean exactly? All of them? Only some of them?' 'What are the criteria for kicking them out of the country? Is it in response to something they've done? Or is the fact that they or their parents were born in another country enough?'

I'd be very curious to hear his argument in response. What sort of logic does it follow? If you can get into a conversation with Danny and make him feel that you genuinely want to understand his way of thinking without immediately wanting to change it, then you can go a step further and try to stretch his thinking a little, invite him to explore his ideas and substantiate them. 'If all foreigners have to leave because they were not born here, what about your friends? I know you get along well with Amir. He wasn't born here and, by your criteria, that makes him a foreigner. So that would mean kicking him out, too. How would that work exactly?'

Refraining from an active disagreement is not the same as approving of or agreeing with the view expressed. Yet that's a pitfall we often tumble into: unless I go on the offensive, I'm tacitly agreeing with what's been said. Our tendency is to reach into our magic top hat and conjure up a host of opinions to bedazzle or berate the other person, but that simply doesn't work and can often lead to increased polarisation. The other person just becomes more and more convinced that they are right, and so do you. And with no one listening, the pair of you might as well be voices crying in the wilderness.

The Socratic response can add depth to many a discussion or difference of opinion. At the very least, it provides flexibility: you extend your thinking beyond your own point of view and allow yourself to be enriched by another perspective. In the example above, a series of well-calibrated Socratic questions may well give Danny some new insights, or at least confront him with the limits of his own statement. That in itself is a valuable development and not one you'll achieve simply by spluttering, 'You can't say that!'

ENDURING IRRITATION

People aren't always in the mood to be questioned about the views they express. Training your Socratic attitude usually involves not reacting in the way people expect you to. You don't chat along pleasantly, you don't offer advice, you don't necessarily respond empathically with familiar affirmations. This can sometimes prompt an irritated response. And that's okay. There's no traction without friction, right? When irritation arises, it's often because you've asked a question that's got someone thinking. Or you've made a good point. At times it means you have to swallow hard and brace yourself. The other person can very easily take their irritation out on you.

*

I remember adopting a Socratic attitude in a conversation with my mum and prompting just such an irritated outburst. I'd gone to Mexico on holiday and didn't call to let her know I'd arrived safely. Mother was not best pleased.

'It's only right that a child should call their parents when they go on holiday!' she insisted.

I sat there in full-on Socratic mode: instead of responding empathically, I was curious as to where this value judgement of hers was coming from. Without trying to defend myself, I genuinely wondered if it was true that 'It's only right that a child should call their parents when they go on holiday.' I asked what was making her angry, about the ideas behind her assumption, the whys and wherefores of this filial duty. My calm response must have triggered even more annoyance, because after a while she burst out in exasperation, 'Can't you just have a normal conversation?'

I responded – surprise, surprise – with a question. What did she understand by the term 'normal conversation'?

'You know ... normal! With emotions and stuff!'

This exchange taught me two things:

1. People often qualify a conversation as 'normal' when emotions are expressed. But it's worth asking whether that's really the case, and whether those emotions actually help you in your conversation.
2. If someone expects or needs empathy and doesn't get it, this often results in disappointment and frustration.

So you always have the option of responding with empathy and understanding to start with, and then transitioning into a more Socratic dialogue by asking questions. If you decide not to do that and stick to asking questions in a spirit of curiosity and wonder, then you have no choice but to accept the other person's irritation for what it is: part of the process and not to be taken personally.

THE STRUCTURE OF A SOCRATIC DISCUSSION

In the world of business and in the wider world of arts and cultural centres, the term 'Socratic discussion' is popping up with increasing regularity. The starting point for this book is both the attitude that you train by having this type of exchange and the structure of the Socratic discussion itself. It's a structure that can help you ask very incisive and relevant questions. Reading this book may not instantly enable you to follow every nuance of such a discussion and master all the techniques, but it will help you understand the sort of thing you can expect, once you start practising your new-found questioning skills.

A Socratic discussion is a meeting of minds, an exploratory conversation about our thought processes, in which the participants investigate what they think and why they think it. The goal, once again, is wisdom. What do we mean when we use certain concepts? What do we think of a given situation? It's not a discussion in which we try to convince someone else or defend our own opinion, but an open investigation into 'what is the case', looking out for hidden presuppositions and working towards wisdom. Our words and ideas are brought into sharper focus by those of others. And the result is often a more confident, shared vision.

The Socratic discussion is a way to arrive at wisdom together, by endlessly questioning each other's statements. Many such discussions are now carried out in organisations and recreational settings: at major banks and health centres, among doctors and lawyers, in groups of friends and even in prisons. The nature of the method lends itself to a wide range of applications and sections of society.

The process of a Socratic dialogue

A Socratic dialogue has a fixed structure, borrowed from the approach taken by Socrates around 2,500 years ago. This encompasses a number of key principles. It's important to be familiar with these principles because they are inherent in asking good questions, developing a philosophical attitude and searching for shared, true knowledge. The better prepared you are, the easier it will be to remain true to your own instincts and trust in your own questions.

A Socratic dialogue is an exploration that starts from a single philosophical question

A Socratic dialogue centres on a single philosophical question, one that is relevant to the whole group. The kind of question a Google search isn't going to help you with. The answer can't be found on Wikipedia, in the columns of a newspaper or on the pages of a lifestyle magazine. It's the kind of question you can only explore by becoming wiser together, by thinking long and hard and by asking other questions. And by formulating answers, questioning them and exploring new concepts as you go.

In your conversation with others, your own view becomes more clearly defined. You train yourself by clearly expressing your point of view in the group discussion, by listening openly and attentively and by asking questions. The question that kicks off a Socratic dialogue always consists of one or more major abstract concepts that the group wants to explore. What is justice? When is it permissible to lie? When should you stop helping? What are medical professionals allowed to decide on a patient's behalf? Can a judge have their own opinion? When is stealing justifiable? All interesting, thought-provoking questions with the power to trigger emotional responses. Questions that open the door to exploring new perspectives, discovering connections and investigating novel ways of thinking.

*

In addition to that one central philosophical question, a Socratic dialogue is conducted on the basis of a single case study brought in by one of the participants: a real-life experience that is focused on throughout the conversation. Life's big concepts such as 'lying', 'justice' and 'cooperation' gain greater meaning when being tested and applied to the practicalities of everyday existence.

It's often not that much of a challenge for us to talk in abstract terms. If I ask a group 'What is lying?', it seldom has trouble coming up with a fairly coherent definition that all the members can more or less agree on. It's possible to answer a question like 'When should you stop helping?' with a general answer that makes sense and sounds impressive enough. But it's a different story when we focus consistently on a specific, real-life situation. Then you start to discover that broad brushstrokes aren't really that much use. You find yourself having to adopt a position, and having to explain it. Does this specific answer in this specific case constitute a lie? Why? Why not? Can this specific action be described as helping? Working with a single example lends a framework and gives greater depth to the conversation.

One Socratic discussion that I led focused on the question 'Should you lie to a friend?' I asked each participant to write down an initial yes-or-no answer and to back it up with an argument. Opinion was divided. Some thought that lying was permissible, to protect the other person or to serve a good cause. Others disagreed and felt that in a real friendship you always tell the truth.

One member of the group, Esther, presented the following case study:

One of my best friends has never had much luck with relationships. She's had boyfriends dump her for no reason, guys who were seeing someone else behind her back, guys who treated her badly – you know the kind of thing. A few weeks ago, she came to visit me, head over heels in love. She had met this guy who was so thoughtful, charming and funny. They had been seeing each other for a few weeks and she was completely besotted with him. She was happier than I had seen her in a long time.

'It turns out he's a friend of a friend of yours,' she added, scrolling on her phone for some photos. When she showed me the pictures, I had to bite my tongue. I recognised his face and knew him by name and by reputation. Friends had told me he always had a few girls on the go and that he had been in trouble with the police. 'Well?' my best friend asked. 'What do you think?'

I didn't have the heart to tell her the truth. In the end, all I said was, 'Yeah, I do know him, but only vaguely. He seems like a really nice guy. I'm glad you're so happy together.'

This is when things get really interesting. Is this lying? And is it okay to lie in this situation? And, while we're at it, can we call this a genuine friendship? Why? Why not? The group explored this specific case and examined the concepts associated with it: lying, truth, friendship, conditionality, loyalty, protection, relationship and more. Diving deeply into this one case allowed them to examine their viewpoints more clearly in relation to one another. The participants really had to pool their thought processes, delve into the other person's point of view, ask question after question and explore the subtleties of the situation. All in search of wisdom.

At the end of the discussion I asked everyone to take another look at their own initial yes-or-no answer to the question 'Should you lie to a friend?' Would they still express their view in the same way? Or would they rephrase it? No one stuck to the answer they had written down at first. Through the discussion they had just had, concepts had taken on a new meaning, nuances and connections had become clearer and they were better able to see where the heart of the matter lay, in their own eyes at least.

The upshot of a Socratic discussion goes well beyond 'Yeah, well, we bounced around a few ideas for a while and eventually worked out what it was all about.' It goes on to generate even more opportunities for exploration and enquiry. You continue to discover new concepts worth questioning and new associations to ponder, and the philosophical attitude and skills you have been working towards start to come more naturally to you.

A Socratic discussion doesn't start from definitions

Often, when I lead a Socratic discussion, someone starts by saying, 'Yes, but shouldn't we begin by defining what we mean by vision/justice/courage/friendship/lying/helping?'

It's understandable, of course: there's an undeniable appeal in working with a nice solid definition that gives us a sense of control and something to hold on to. But in a Socratic discussion it tends to be counter-productive. In fact, it doesn't do you any good at all. Concepts and labels only take on meaning when you attach them to something.

A Socratic discussion that I remember well involved teachers and school administrators. The question we took as our starting point was 'When does a vision get in the way?' The everyday scenario we looked at was supplied by a primary-school teacher called Lara. She worked at a school that had formulated a very clear vision on art education. This vision had a strong focus on the artistic process, with a clear emphasis on autonomy and ownership on the part of the pupils. The teacher's role was limited to supervising and gently guiding the process, not dictating it or directing it. A new teacher had just been hired to teach a class of six- to seven-year-olds. At her job interview she said she shared that vision completely, and that she was open-minded and eager to learn. In practice, however, the opposite was true: the open-minded new teacher turned out to be stuck in her ways and gave traditional lessons on prescribed themes. In other words, she appeared to be ignoring the school's vision altogether. At the time Lara's view was that the school's vision was actually more of a hindrance than a help. Both for the new teacher and for the staff as a whole.

The scene had been set for the rest of the group to explore. Did the school really have a vision? Was that vision getting in the way? And who was getting in the way of the vision? The new teacher? The teachers as a whole? Or just Lara? We were about to start exploring these issues when another teacher stopped the discussion and said, 'But shouldn't we define what we mean by "vision" first? Perhaps we all have a different idea of what it actually means!'

She wasn't wrong. Each member of the group might well have had a different idea of what constitutes a vision. But that's something they'll find out along the way when they start applying the concept to the case that Lara presented. Fall into the 'definition trap' and hours can fly by while you wrestle with abstract theories of what does and doesn't qualify as a vision. Or the opposite happens: someone formulates what sounds like a perfectly acceptable definition and everyone more or less agrees with it, but within five minutes you have to start revising your definition because it doesn't quite fit the situation. A Socratic discussion never starts by defining concepts. Instead it sets out to discover what concepts mean by applying them, as opposed to fencing them off with general definitions.

Another regular occurrence: after the break, someone returns to a Socratic discussion beaming with pride, smartphone in hand. 'Problem solved! I looked it up in the *OED*. Listen, here's what it says about justice/courage/helping/pride …' These days my standard response is: 'And what do *you* think? Is the *OED* right? Does what it says apply to this situation?'

We make statements all day long. We sum up what we think of a certain situation. 'He shouldn't have lied, under those circumstances.' 'People who speak with their mouths full are disrespectful of others.' 'Olga is a joy to work with.' Yet when you take a stand on a particular issue, it's often not clear what your position is based on. Your verdict is like a punchline without the rest of the joke: we don't yet know why you think that person shouldn't have lied, why people who speak with food in their mouth are disrespectful, or what's so great about working with Olga.

Having a Socratic discussion enables you to discover exactly what lies behind these statements. You discover judgements, values, arguments and assumptions about human nature that, in some cases, you didn't even know you had. As a result, a Socratic discussion is a bit like pressing rewind on a person's thought processes: someone makes a statement about reality and, by asking questions that take you behind that statement, you work your way back to the arguments on which it is based.

'Olga is a joy to work with.'

'What's so great about working with Olga?'

'Well, for one thing, she's always on time.'

'So punctuality makes someone a joy to work with?'

'Yes, as a matter of fact, I think it does. Olga is punctual and that makes her a joy to work with.'

While 'punctuality' is a defining argument for one person, it needn't be for someone else. They may think Olga's a joy to work with because she's friendly, bakes apple pie for the whole team every now and again or because she makes a good strong pot of coffee.

When we nod in agreement at a statement like 'Olga's a joy to work with', 'We make a really good team' or 'What Jack did was inexcusable', there's no guarantee that we mean the same thing at all.

In a Socratic discussion people work towards a consensus

As you develop your questioning attitude, one of the most important things to keep at the back of your mind is: working towards a consensus. Very often we end up in a tug-of-war rather than an open discussion, carried along by our determination to convince the other person. More than anything, we want them to see things our way.

Working towards a consensus may sound a bit namby-pamby, but it's not. It's not about simply making concessions and scrambling to reach the apparent safety of the middle ground. Nor is it about leaving things in the middle and agreeing to disagree. Working towards a consensus means that you keep on searching. That you keep looking for nuances, for the outer limits of various concepts and their interpretations, for differences and similarities. All too often our conversations grind to a halt just when things are getting interesting, when the differences are becoming clear. Suddenly we bail out, put our findings to a majority vote or settle for those good old standbys 'This is my truth' or 'You're entitled to your opinion.'

'My truth' and 'your opinion' are the death knell for a good, in-depth and perhaps even philosophical conversation. If practical philosophy is about the desire to become wiser and the search for shared, true knowledge, then that knowledge has to rise above and go beyond everyone's personal experience. 'This is how I feel about things' is not a statement about reality and is not an argument we can examine together, and so the question 'Is this true?' is always central to a joint search for wisdom.

A remark like that falls short of dealing with reality and does nothing more than describe one person's individual feelings about things. Responding to a statement like 'I just feel that Ibrahim was completely within his rights to act that way', you're not going to get much further than 'Okay, thanks for sharing.' The same goes for a statement like 'I don't think we worked together effectively on this project.' This is a clear statement of feeling or opinion, but you cannot explore the reality of such a statement together and there's little point in gauging the truth of a feeling or an opinion. Unless they're deliberately out to mislead us about how they feel or what they believe, of course it's true when someone says, 'This is how I feel' and equally true when they say, 'I believe that …'

Statements such as 'Ibrahim acted fairly' or 'There was no effective cooperation in this project' *can* be questioned and examined. You can take a closer look at how people did or didn't work together and whether or not it was effective, as well as establishing why. You can find out exactly how Ibrahim acted and assess whether it was fair. A feeling or an opinion is a private matter. Feel free to have them and share them, but don't enter them into a philosophical conversation as research material, because they won't be any use at all.

Working towards a consensus is very much about the question 'Is this claim true?' And that only makes sense if those claims are actual claims about the real world, not subjective opinions. It's also worth noting that working towards a consensus is different from actually achieving a consensus. Achieving doesn't really matter all that much; what counts in a Socratic discussion is the work you put in. The aim and the driving force behind the discussion: the desire to keep on searching, from a position of not-knowing and in a spirit of curiosity.

Miriam van Reijen, a fellow practical philosopher, told me about a Socratic discussion she once led. The case they chose to discuss was brought in by a father and concerned his daughter. The daughter wasn't in a good place: crippled by debt, destructive relationships and a drug addiction. The father tried to help his daughter by giving her money. Occasionally at first, but eventually as a monthly payment. He hoped it would help her get her life back on track. It didn't. He found out that the money was being spent on drugs and ended up stopping his payments, but only after five years.

The Socratic examination then dealt with the question 'When should you stop helping?' One participant said that in this case the father should have stopped helping a lot sooner. Another disagreed: 'No, you should never stop helping your own child.' Everyone had their own idea of when you should stop helping. Miriam explained, 'In the end, the consensus we reached – more or less – wasn't found in the case itself, but at another, broader level: we eventually concluded that you should stop when the helping no longer helps.'

This is an example where a consensus could not be found at a concrete level, but fell into place at a more abstract level. And even then, there's more to question and more to discover. At what point in this case did the helping stop being helpful? And who gets to decide when something isn't helping: the helper or the recipient? Ask a few more questions and the consensus you thought you had reached is almost sure to fall away. And that's why *working towards* a consensus is so important. It keeps the conversation moving forward, keeps the engine running, ensures that the process is one of investigation and that the participants are keen to continue. But when you stop working towards a consensus and start trying to *achieve* one, before you know it, your discussion will have devolved into a polarised debate or a spot of random chit-chat.

Exercise: keep on searching for a consensus

Have a conversation with someone, starting from a question that neither of you has an answer to and that you both think is worth exploring. 'Can you lie to a friend?' might be a good one to start with. Begin by asking for an example: have you ever lied to a friend? Did you feel justified at the time? Why did lying seem like the right thing to do? Would that lie have been right under any circumstances?

Set out to discover new insights, not to convince the other person that you are right. It helps if you decide not to focus on your own opinion for a while, but simply to listen to what the other person has to say. Listen sincerely to their point of view and then express your own, concisely and clearly.

Then keep on searching for a consensus together. Where do your views overlap? Where do they differ? Can these differences be bridged?

Accept that you don't have to reach a consensus. Working towards it is the most important thing. You may well find yourself drifting from 'searching for a consensus' into attempting to convince, or you might notice that you've stopped thinking collectively and have started defending your own opinions. When you become aware of this, check in with yourself. What was it that made you abandon the search for a consensus and become more defensive? How can you avoid that next time?

Here are a few ideas for questions you might start with:

- When is violence justified?
- Should we help those in need?
- When is a question out of line?
- Do you always have to be honest?
- Is theft necessarily immoral?
- Is it ever acceptable not to respect someone else's boundaries?

As you develop your questioning skills, you are bound to encounter the same things Socrates did: resistance, *elenchus* and *aporia*. We'll explore these last two terms in more detail over the next few pages, and although they may sound like tropical diseases, their meanings are a little less scary.

Elenchus

A key element in Socrates's dialogues is *elenchus*, which means 'refutation', but comes from the Greek for 'to put to shame'[9] or 'look at with scrutiny'. We think we know all kinds of things for sure. Socrates believed that before you can learn anything, you first have to unlearn what you think you know but do not actually know. The underlying principle of his method was that you can achieve real knowledge by means of not-knowing. A kind of 'testing of thought', of not-knowing and being aware of not-knowing. As Socrates saw it, this was necessary in order to achieve a more substantial and in-depth clarification of an issue.

We all have a vast stockpile of judgements, ideas, beliefs, values and norms that determine our behaviour. But they don't necessarily add up to a consistent whole. Some are made up of norms and values that we have picked up along the way, often courtesy of our parents or teachers, and they come complete with blind spots, unconscious assumptions, distortions and false beliefs, many of them contradictory. In his discussions, Socrates began by trying to bring these contradictions to light by testing and scrutinising them through clever questioning, in order to show the person he was talking to that their existing ideas were inadequate. This refutation, or *elenchus*, often left people feeling ashamed or embarrassed, as they became aware that much of what they believed in – and had just defended tooth and nail – was in fact nonsense.

Speaking in his own defence in the case that the Athenians brought against him, Socrates says:

Chaerephon [...] went to Delphi and boldly asked the oracle to tell him whether [...] there was any one wiser than I was, and the Pythian prophetess answered that there was no man wiser. [...]

When I heard the answer, I said to myself, What can the god mean? and what is the interpretation of his riddle? For I know that I have no wisdom, small or great. [...] And yet he is a god, and cannot lie; that would be against his nature. After long consideration, I at last thought of a method of trying the question. I reflected that if I could only find a man wiser than myself, then I might go to the god with a refutation in my hand. I should say to him, 'Here is a man who is wiser than I am; but you said that I was the wisest.' Accordingly I went to one who had the reputation of wisdom, and observed him – his name I need not mention; he was a politician whom I selected for examination – and the result was as follows: When I began to talk with him, I could not help thinking that he was not really wise, although he was thought wise by many, and wiser still by himself; and thereupon I tried to explain to him that he thought himself wise, but was not really wise; and the consequence was that he hated me, and his enmity was shared by several who were present and heard me.

So I left him, saying to myself, as I went away: Well, although I do not suppose that either of us knows anything really beautiful and good, I am better off than he is, – for he knows nothing, and thinks that he knows; I neither know nor think that I know.[10]

Socrates did the same with writers and artisans, and his experience was always the same: he went looking for someone who had greater insight and knowledge than himself, and he cross-examined them. No matter who they were, they were soon tripped up by his questions and were forced to admit that in fact they didn't quite know exactly what they were talking about when it came to justice, piety, beauty or whatever their supposed area of expertise was. Through this process Socrates demonstrated the other person's unknowingness, which led to refutation or *elenchus*, and the painful realisation that they weren't as knowledgeable as they thought they were. Since this wasn't quite the outcome they had been expecting from their conversation with Socrates, he ended up rubbing a lot of people up the wrong way. Over time, Socrates came to the conclusion that people who are told they know a lot about a particular subject start to think that they are just as much of an authority on a host of other subjects, too:

> I observed that even the good artisans fell into the same error as the poets; – because they were good workmen they thought that they also knew all sorts of high matters, and this defect in them overshadowed their wisdom – therefore I asked myself on behalf of the oracle, whether I would like to be as I was, neither having their knowledge nor their ignorance, or like them in both; and I made answer to myself and to the oracle that I was better off as I was.[11]

Elenchus is a moment in the conversation when it becomes tangible that our initial presuppositions, our opening statements, often turn out to be built on quicksand. Only once this truth has been dredged up and laid on the table is there room to have a discussion that will really get us somewhere. Socrates was convinced that there is only room for real knowledge once you know you don't know. You might say that he started by cleaning out the attic, sweeping away the cobwebs and throwing open a window. This not only confronted people with what a mess their thinking had actually been, but also let in the clear light of day – not to mention some fresh air – and created space for new, true knowledge to emerge.

It's important to know what *elenchus* is. When you develop a questioning attitude and start to wonder about things that seem self-evident, sooner or later you are bound to run into contradictions in the other person's story. You find yourself questioning things that, to the other person, appear so obvious it seems 'weird' to question them.

As we saw in Part One, our convictions are often woven into our identity. So calling those convictions into question, even in ways that seem quite minor, is not likely to make you a whole lot of friends right away. A sense of shame lurks just below the surface of not-knowing and there's every chance that the person on the receiving end of your questions will feel a bit uncomfortable, if only for a short while. Not that this is necessarily a bad thing: the flourishing of new, fruitful and interesting thinking often follows a good pruning back of old ideas.

There were times, especially when I had just been trained in the Socratic attitude, when my questioning made people feel uncomfortable to the point where they started projecting their feelings onto me. 'Christ, you're making everything so complicated!' 'There's no need to play dumb!' 'Stop trying to catch me out with wordplay – you get the idea, right?' These are just some of the responses that knocked me sideways at the time. Now when someone comes out with statements like that, I know it means we're getting somewhere. They tend to arise when the other person starts to sense that they're no longer being entirely coherent. A sure sign that they are moving closer to that uncomfortable state of not-knowing.

There's a good reason why Socrates often asked people's permission before engaging them in conversation. When *elenchus* got them angry and had them blaming him or wanting to pull out of the conversation, Socrates could always remind them what they had agreed to. There's a nice example in the following extract from a conversation between Socrates and Protagoras. At one point it all gets a little too much for Protagoras and he wants to shrug off the conversation with an 'Oh, whatever. Let's just assume for a moment that holiness and justice are the same thing and get on with it …' As this is a book all about philosophical conversations, I have taken the liberty of presenting these quotes, from *The Dialogues of Plato*, in dialogue form:

> PROTAGORAS: I cannot simply agree, Socrates, to the proposition that justice is holy and that holiness is just, for there appears to me to be a difference between them. But what matter? if you please, I please; and let us assume, if you will, that justice is holy, and that holiness is just.
>
> SOCRATES: Pardon me, I do not want this 'if you wish' or 'if you will' sort of argument to be proven, but I want you and me to be proven: I mean to say that the argument will be best proven if there be no 'if'.[12]

Developing your inner Socrates can bring you much wisdom, but it comes at a price: people don't always welcome your line of enquiry.

Dealing with responses to elenchus

When you enter into a conversation and ask question after question, be alert to the kind of phrases I have mentioned above:

- You're making everything needlessly complicated!
- That goes without saying!
- Look, that's just the way things are, okay?

When reactions like that begin to pop up, you know that pursuing your enquiries can lead to a fascinating and worthwhile conversation, but only if you proceed carefully and with the other person's consent. If you sense them becoming irritated or frustrated, you can always ask whether they wish to continue with the discussion or call it a day. If you have asked permission beforehand and the other person has consented to enter into this spot of philosophical exploration, you can always remind them of your earlier agreement and confirm that they are happy to continue. Once they have agreed to press on, your task now is to persist in your Socratic attitude and keep asking attentive and focused questions:

- What is it that I'm making needlessly complicated?
- Why does that go without saying?
- Why is that the way things are?

Aporia

Socratic conversations often end in *aporia*: an all-encompassing feeling of doubt, of not-knowing where you stand any more. The question remains a question, and there's not a single answer that appears satisfactory. The ideas and thoughts you arrive at in your joint exploration are often numerous, without being conclusive or definitive.

The aim of Socratic questioning is not to find another answer that you can cling to, one that does away with the need to think. Every 'answer' you come across in a Socratic conversation is an invitation to keep on asking. It's only by continuing to question that your thinking can remain fluid. It's the search itself – the awareness of how little you actually know – that gives you infinite freedom. When, spurred on by curiosity, you keep on thinking and questioning even what appears to be obvious, there comes a point when you feel that you really don't know *the* definitive answer to anything. But that sense of not-knowing achieved through determined enquiry leaves your thinking with a much stronger foundation than it had before: after all, you have examined, questioned and explored the matter at hand from all sides. *Aporia* is perplexing, but it also sets you free.

You can also encounter *aporia* when you question friends, family or colleagues, strangers in the pub or on the street. After a joint search for truth, someone throws their hands in the air and sighs, 'I just don't know any more! I've looked at this from all kinds of different angles and a lot of them seem to be worthwhile. But now I simply feel confused!' There's nothing wrong with that. Quite the contrary, in fact: you've been confronted with how little you really know. And that awareness is key to developing a questioning Socratic attitude. That awareness, that deflated feeling of *aporia* – of 'I just don't know any more' – is in fact the starting point for something valuable: asking a good question. As the philosophical practitioner Harm van der Gaag writes, 'When you don't know something and *know* you don't know something, you have two options: you can say something. Or you can ask a question.'[13]

Exercise: go in search of aporia

Invite someone to question you about a conviction you have. Tell them to keep on asking questions and to be critical of what you say. If all goes according to plan, you'll soon arrive at the limits of what you know for sure and have no choice but to say, 'Goodness, I really don't know.' Beforehand you might find yourself coming out with a statement like 'That's just the way it is.' And the next question – 'Why is it that way?' – is one you don't have an answer to. Welcome to *aporia*! Take a moment to experience it. You might feel a little odd, a little uneasy, but at the same time the world is at your feet. See if you can revel in this brave new world of 'I don't know.' After all, didn't we decide that we wanted to endure ignorance and embrace not-knowing? Well, that moment has arrived. What questions come to mind?

Now that you know the ingredients that make up a Socratic discussion, you are more prepared to train yourself in asking better, sharper questions. Knowing what *elenchus* is, how *aporia* feels and how you can respond to them can be a big help. This level of awareness only makes things more fun, more interesting and more challenging.

In this section you have discovered what a Socratic attitude entails and how to develop one. It takes courage, wonder and a willingness to revel in not-knowing. You are ready to practise empathic neutrality and train your Socratic response. You are prepared for what you might encounter when you engage in conversations from this Socratic angle: the uneasy feeling of *aporia* and the irritation that comes with *elenchus* are feelings that you are going to have to endure. It's also important to notice when someone else is experiencing *elenchus* or *aporia* and check that they're happy to proceed before pushing ahead with more questions. You know that a Socratic conversation starts from a philosophical question and a real-life case study, and that working towards a consensus – as opposed to trying to achieve one – is an essential driving force behind an open and equal quest for truth.

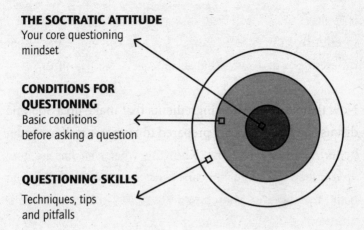

THE SOCRATIC ATTITUDE
Your core questioning
mindset

**CONDITIONS FOR
QUESTIONING**
Basic conditions
before asking a question

QUESTIONING SKILLS
Techniques, tips
and pitfalls

The above diagram encapsulates my approach to the art of asking questions. Your core, the main foundation, is the Socratic attitude. Once that core is firmly in place and forms the wellspring for your questions, you can move on to the second ring: conditions for questioning. And once you've developed a more Socratic attitude and the conditions for questioning are right, you can set about honing your skills with practical techniques, tips and pitfalls. These conditions are important and, all too often, we tend to focus solely on the outer ring. There are countless well-meaning articles and courses that provide questioning techniques, yet overlook the crucial attitude behind the question and fail to consider whether the right conditions are in place.

PART THREE

Conditions for questioning

Don't explain your philosophy. Embody it.

Epictetus[1]

L ET'S SAY YOU'VE mastered the Socratic curious attitude you've been seeking. You are familiar with the ingredients of a discursive enquiry and you know how to handle them. The bases are covered, your foundation is solid. You're at one with wonder and steer clear of snap judgements and automatic empathy. Now what? How can you establish a setting that enables you to carry out a Socratic exploration with someone? What do you have to take into account before you can put the art of questioning into practice? What skills are going to help you come up with good questions?

CONDITION ONE

It all begins with being a good listener

Good questions are questions about the other person. A good question sticks to the story they are telling, the experience they are sharing. When I ask a question, there should be no undercurrent pulling the conversation around to me, to how *I* feel about things, what *I* think. Yet despite our best intentions, that's exactly what happens a lot of the time, and this has everything to do with our ability to listen. We're all fairly bad listeners, and we only listen half the time. If we're not drifting off or making a shopping list while the other person is talking, then we're thinking about what we're going to say next or imagining how we might behave in the situation they are describing. This approach to listening is almost certain to generate a question that is not about the other person, but about yourself. If you want to ask a question that's genuinely relevant to the other person, you have to learn to really listen first.

Good listening – listening purely and simply, and without inserting your own interpretations or assumptions or opinions – is not as easy as it sounds. It takes practice. Once you succeed in listening without superimposing your own narrative on what you are hearing, you'll find it becomes easier to concentrate on the other person's story. You'll be much better able to form a mental picture of what they are telling you, and questions that lead to a deeper understanding will start to come naturally.

To help develop your listening skills, let's start by focusing on your intentions as a listener.

Intention is everything

There are roughly three intentions, or positions, of listening:

1. The first position puts the 'I' in intention and can be summed up by the phrase 'What do I make of this?' Listen this way and you keep wondering what you would do, think, feel or say in the given situation. 'How would I have tackled that?' 'What would I have said?' You're not engaged with the feelings, thoughts or experiences of the speaker, but instead with your own point of view and your own opinions or ideas. Listening with this intention all too often triggers the fix, help or advice reflex or sees you gearing up to share your own story. Any questions you ask are likely to be suggestive, judgemental or leading. 'Don't you think he's right?' 'Wouldn't you rather visit the islands instead of heading south?' These questions mainly indicate how *you* feel about the subject of the conversation and cast the other person in a supporting role.

2. The second position is the 'You' intention. I like to characterise this as the 'What exactly do you mean?' approach to listening. If you listen with this intention, you listen curiously and Socratically: you know that

there are all kinds of things you don't know. You are fully aware that the other person's experiences aren't necessarily the same as yours and so you keep your focus on them. 'What do you mean, exactly?' 'What were you thinking?' 'How did you feel when …?' 'What exactly do you mean by …?' With this approach, you put yourself into the other person's mind as much as you can. You want to understand their story and way of thinking, and get to grips with and question their logic. Not for a second are you trying to convince the other person or give them advice. You're not itching to tell them what they could have done differently or how you would have tackled things. The questions you ask, when listening from this position, are often ones that dig deeper: that either give you more factual information about the situation being described or offer greater insight into how the other person experienced that situation. They are attentive questions that stick close to the other person and their story.

3. Third up is the 'We' intention. I like to call it the 'How are we doing?' position. This is actually a kind of meta-position, hovering above the conversation and looking down on it. Listening in from this position, you observe yourself and the other person from a distance, as partners in the conversation. You register how you're feeling, how your partner appears to be doing. From this position you may suddenly become aware that you are

talking in circles, that every sentence starts with 'but', or that the other person is not really answering your question at all but heading off at a tangent. You also notice how both of you are doing, non-verbally. You might see the other person fidgeting all the time, or feel your muscles tightening up during your conversation.

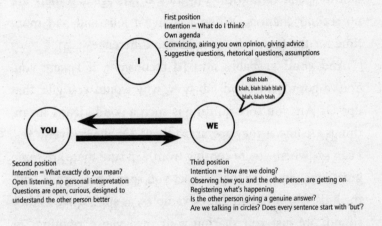

First position
Intention = What do I think?
Own agenda
Convincing, airing you own opinion, giving advice
Suggestive questions, rhetorical questions, assumptions

Blah blah blah, blah blah blah, blah, blah blah

Second position
Intention = What exactly do you mean?
Open listening, no personal interpretation
Questions are open, curious, designed to understand the other person better

Third position
Intention = How are we doing?
Observing how you and the other person are getting on
Registering what's happening
Is the other person giving a genuine answer?
Are we talking in circles? Does every sentence start with 'but'?

The three listening intentions in one example

Imagine you are talking to a good friend. They tell you, 'I just don't know what to do about my job. All the enjoyment has gone out of it and the commute is getting me down. I'm never home in time to put the kids to bed. Sometimes I think I should quit, but I just don't dare. I mean, it pays well and I work with a decent bunch of people. What should I do?'

*

If you're listening from the first position, you may well be *thinking*, 'Stay put, that's what you should do! You've got it made at that place: great salary, good team and only half an hour's drive away. I would be so lucky, if I were in your position! My commute is much longer and I earn less than you!' Or you might think, 'Sure, quit! Why wait? It's important to spend time with your kids at this age and there are no second chances. When I changed jobs and had more time for the family, it made all the difference.'

And you'd probably *say*: 'I'd reconsider, if I were you. You've got a very good job now, why would you give that up? Or 'Are you sure quitting is such a good idea? I mean, things are fine as they are, aren't they?' Or alternatively, 'Yes, I can see where you're coming from. I'm sure there are some great jobs out there that will let you spend more time with the kids.' However, all these examples, as supportive as they sound, are just you sharing your own views, opinions or concerns. These responses do not engage with the character, priorities, wishes or desires of your friend.

When you listen from the second position, with the intention of getting inside the other person's mind, you *think* in terms of questions. 'How is this situation working out for you?' 'What are you thinking?' 'What are you feeling?' 'Do your thoughts and feelings change from time to time?' 'What does your partner think about this?'

From the second position you might *say* those thoughts exactly as you thought them: 'How is this situation working out for you?' 'What are you thinking?' 'What are you feeling?' Note the simplicity of these questions, and how your thoughts and speech share the same focus and echo one another exactly.

In other words, you immerse yourself in the other person's experience, without holding up an experience of your own by way of comparison. There is no attempt to fix things, smooth them over or play them down. This requires self-control; the tendency to blurt out your own story, give your own view or impart your own wisdom can be very strong.

To ask good questions, it's important to train yourself to listen from this second position – the 'You' position – with the intention of finding out exactly what the other person means. We have the habit of listening from the 'I' position, with the intention of working out how we might solve a problem if we were in the other person's shoes. 'What-exactly-do-you-mean?' listening might seem like more of an effort, but it's not. Once you get the knack, you'll notice that it makes for much cleaner and calmer communication: it's just 'plain' listening to the other person's story, without having to interpose your own opinions, ideas or understanding of what's being said. Your mind will start to quieten down.

*

Finally, if you're listening from the third position, your intent is to *register* how your conversation partner is doing, the nature of your contact with each other, and what you can read in their body language. You also pick up on verbal signals, like your partner starting every other sentence with 'Yes, but …'

You might *say*, 'When you talk about your current job, your face relaxes and you look happy. When you talk about leaving, you cross your arms and look away.' Or 'I've noticed that a lot of your answers start with "Yes, but …." What do you think that means?' We'll explore this third approach in greater detail in the next section.

Exercise: switch your listening position

Next time someone tells you about something they have experienced, start by deliberately listening with the first intention: what do *I* make of all this? Pay attention to what you think, what you say and how the other person reacts. Then make a conscious effort to shift your listening to the second position: what exactly do *you* mean? Regard your own judgement and opinion as totally uninteresting, and simply immerse yourself in the other person's story. What happens to your thinking? What kind of things do you say? What effect does this have on the connection between you?

CONDITION TWO

Take language seriously

Our thinking is a whirl of images, sounds, words and emotions. But if we want to convey our thoughts to someone else, we mainly stick to words. Words are the main vehicle for our thinking and communication, and therefore for our questions. All too often we take a very casual approach to language. 'This word, that word, what does it really matter?' we sigh. 'You get what I mean, don't you?' That's a pity, and a poorly chosen word often causes confusion and static on the line when you're trying to have a rewarding discussion. By using language cleanly and clearly, by choosing your words carefully, you're able to clarify the conversation and ask better questions, and you become more sensitive to what the other person is actually saying. It's not always an accident when a person uses one particular word rather than a similar word with a different shade of meaning. By becoming more sensitive to language, your hearing becomes more acute in terms of what is and isn't being said, what gets swept under the carpet and which words or concepts someone prefers to avoid. And that in itself can be an enormously rich resource for your good questions.

A while back, I taught a course called 'Philosophy in Everyday Life'. I asked the participants to write down what they wanted to learn, in the form of a question. For example, one person wrote, 'How can I learn to think in a more structured way?' Another asked, 'How can I bring more depth to my conversations?'

One question someone wrote was 'Where can I find focus?' It may seem like a tiny nuance or even a slip of the pen, but the fact that a person asks *where* rather than *how* they can find focus may well reveal something interesting about them. It could be that they see focus as something to be found outside themselves, rather than the result of an internal process. The unconscious nature of these subtle differences in word choice makes them interesting things to pick apart.

We can give away our true intentions with the smallest of words. Take the words 'but' and 'so', for example. The question 'Have you discussed this with Emily?' is fundamentally different from 'But have you discussed this with Emily?' or 'So you've discussed this with Emily?'

Another example is the negative formulation. Turning the question around and asking, 'Haven't you discussed this with Emily yet?' immediately leaves someone the feeling that you think they should have talked to Emily a long time ago.

By using negative constructions, or sneaking in a 'so' or a 'but', we often give away our hand without realising it. Whether the other person consciously picks up on it or not, the resulting question often comes across as far less open than it might seem.

Like Sherlock

This is the level of detail at which Sherlock Holmes exercises his powers of reasoning: he examines, observes, infers and draws conclusions. A blond hair on a jacket, scratches on a phone, a seemingly forgotten hat on a coat rack ... Treat them as clues and they can tell you all kinds of things about a person. In Sherlock's case, whether or not they are innocent, a thief or a cold-blooded killer. Just as Sherlock uses his powers of observation and inductive reasoning, picking up on subtle clues and using them to solve seemingly impossible cases, so we can do the same with words and language. What someone does or doesn't say, the words they do or don't use can provide us with insights into how they structure their thoughts.

Now, you may be thinking, 'Does there always have to be a deeper meaning? I mean, don't most of us just say whatever words occur to us at the time? Maybe there's nothing behind them at all.' That may be true. But I would argue it is way more fun to entertain the possibility that we don't just pick our words at random. It gives us much more to explore, think about and learn. If you assume that language is simply a random scattering of words and sentences, life becomes that much duller. You stop paying attention, stop wondering why someone might have opted for one word and not the other. You deprive yourself of an important route into unconscious patterns of thought, beliefs and assumptions.

Language and surface listening

I've talked a lot about the importance of depth in this book when it comes to your own thinking and Socratic discussions, but a good way to hone your listening skills and zero in on how someone uses language is a technique called 'surface listening'. This is done not by being empathic or by adopting the first or second listening position, but by adopting the third approach and simply by listening Socratically to surface features. This involves tuning into the language someone is using, rather than what that language means. Listening to how something is said rather than what's being said; to its form rather than its content. First, you may note whether someone is asking a question, making an assertion, giving an explanation, defending a statement or putting forward an argument. Then you could listen out for the concepts someone touches on, and whether what they are saying contains contradictions or errors in their argument's logic.

By default, we listen with our imaginative faculties fully activated, and picture ourselves in the other person's situation. Without even realising it, we fill in missing details for ourselves, embellish their sentences, colour in their images. But when you practise surface listening and tune in to form rather than content, you dial down your imagination and engage more with the other person and what they are actually saying.

This way of listening also consumes less energy. It is sometimes referred to as 'active mindfulness', because your attention is completely focused on the other person or, more precisely, on the words and language they are using. You don't fill in or finish off their thought, you make no imaginative corrections or additions. You might call it a form of wilful stupidity. Your intent is to not take the obvious for granted, to assume you don't understand and to express an almost childlike curiosity about what might be behind those words.

Our words can sometimes reveal our contradictions, our hidden assumptions, our faulty thinking. Listening Socratically and tuning in to the surface level of the conversation allows you to pick up on these shortcomings more easily. This technique can be a goldmine when you want to get someone to reflect on their own thinking. It enables you to ask questions that dig deeper and that are firmly focused on what the other person is actually saying. You don't listen to understand, you listen *not* to understand, so that you can work together with the other person to explore what may be behind their words.

Exercise: surface listening

Listen to someone talking about something that happened to them and concentrate on the language they use. Don't engage with what you think they are trying to say, but only with the words you actually hear. Do you notice any contradictions? Does the speaker have a filler word they keep repeating? Do you hear words like 'but', 'not' and 'so'? The main thing is to listen without reaching for any deeper understanding beyond what is actually being said. What do you notice about their speech?

Exercise: don't agree or disagree

The next time you listen to a conversation, do it with the conviction that what you think is totally irrelevant. Listen to the language being used, observe where people contradict themselves, tune in to the logic of their argument and be alert to any dubious reasoning. Listen out for problems in how they're saying what they're saying, elements that they gloss over, arguments that feel baseless or reek of bullshit. Try not to worry about the content and whether you agree with it or not.

When you take yourself out of the conversation like this and put your own opinion to one side, you can discover a lot of valuable things about the other person's thinking. Later on, there's bound to come a point in the conversation when you can say what *you* think and explain your own point of view. But the more you master this way of listening, the less you will probably feel the need to state your own case.

Body language

What about non-verbal communication? How we behave is certainly as important as what we say. As I see it, the art of asking questions is very much about language and developing our sensitivity to it. Body language is also a part of that process. Even when our words are designed to twist, conceal or sweeten the truth, the body is often easier to read. So you have to train your eyes, ears and heart in that respect, too. This is where our third listening position really comes into its own. It enables you to register, as objectively as possible, whether someone is behaving congruently: are their body language and facial expressions chiming with what they are saying?

A woman called Paula came to see me for a philosophical conversation. She had questions about her relationship and had started to wonder whether she wanted to move in with her partner. I asked her what arguments she had for *not* moving in together. Without hesitation, she reeled off her reasons: it would mean sacrificing her independence and adapting to her partner, and she didn't know whether that was something she wanted or was even capable of doing. As she spoke, her face was relaxed and animated, and she did her best to articulate her arguments as clearly as possible and there was music in her voice.

When I asked her for her arguments in favour of living together, she was quiet for a while. Her face tightened, her jaw tensed and she let out a deep sigh. In those five wordless seconds, what she was really thinking became so clear it was almost palpable. Although she hadn't yet formulated her own position, it was child's play for an outsider to read what she really thought about living with her partner.

We sometimes forget how useful it can be to ask questions about non-verbal information. Body language can be a source of essential insights at a moment when a person's feelings are yet to be articulated. Pointing out those telltale signs can help someone become aware of their feelings and start to put them into words.

With Paula, I decided to ask what lay behind her silence, her sigh and her pained expression.

'I didn't even realise I was doing it' was her first reaction.

'What were you thinking when you sighed?' I asked.

'Nothing really. But I felt a bit stressed out. I saw myself alone, sitting quietly on the couch of an evening and Erik coming home and wanting to talk about the hassle at work. Just the idea of it made me feel tired.'

'Do you have any arguments in favour of living together?' I asked.

Again it was quiet for a moment. Paula bit her lip. And because I had just made her aware of what her face and body were communicating, she laughed. 'Ha! I was biting my lip! And then I thought, "Oh, and now she's going to ask me what *that* means." And to be honest, I already know.

It means I can't think of any arguments for living together, even though I'd like to. So maybe I'm just not ready to take that step now.'

A sigh, a silence, shifting uneasily in your seat, biting your lip, closing your eyes, a tightening of the face: these are all answers of a kind and are just as important as the spoken word and sometimes easier and clearer to read. They tell you that your question has triggered something in the other person, because the body's response is often quicker and more honest when a question hits home. This is very useful information and deserves the same prominence in the art of asking questions as the spoken word.

Exercise: an eye for body language

When you engage in surface listening and shelve your empathy, it gives you time and space to observe what the other person is saying with their body. Watch and describe. What impression is the other person giving off? What are they doing with their hands? What does their face tell you? What about their breathing? Do you hear sighs or groans, or is their breathing relaxed? Do they take time to pause? And does their bearing change at that point?

Ask yourself what sorts of things you could pick up from the other person's body language if you didn't speak their language.

CONDITION THREE

Ask permission

Years ago, when I began training to ask better questions by taking courses and workshops, one of my teachers told the group: 'There's an element of "don't try this at home" in what we're doing. Here in the group, we know the score. We know what we want to achieve and the intention behind this endless questioning of ours. But it's worth remembering that very often the last thing people "out there in the real world" want is to face a barrage of questions.'

She was right, of course. But stubborn and naive as I was, I happily ignored her advice. I had fallen in love with asking questions, gaining wisdom and teaming up with others to think about and explore fascinating themes. And as with any new love, I couldn't wait to share the good news with everyone. This new discovery of mine was so great! It was going to make the world a better place and I felt sure that everyone would agree with me.

Pulling on my sneakers, I charged into the fray like a regular Socrates 2.0, launching rapid-fire questions at everyone I met. During family dinners I got on everyone's nerves by not stating my own position but questioning other people's assertions and rebutting them with more questions. Friends could no longer rely on my empathy and consolation when they confided in me about their lovers' quarrel or frustrations at work, but had to put up with a ruthless cross-examination instead. When a salesman cajoled me with 'Look here, lady. If I give you a discount, the whole city will soon be beating down the door!', the poor man was met with a string of questions challenging the truth of his statement. You may be unsurprised to learn that I didn't exactly make myself popular by forcing my new passion on others. Sadder and wiser – the better world I had envisioned was taking a long time to materialise – I forced myself to tone things down a bit. A little less enthusiasm, to say nothing of fanaticism, seemed like the way to go, if I didn't want to end up pining away with only Olle, my cat, for company.

Socrates often explicitly asked his potential conversation partners whether they felt like investigating an issue. He asked them in advance if he could question them. And with good reason. When you invite someone else to enter into an in-depth conversation by explicitly questioning their thoughts on a specific issue, the conversation becomes a shared responsibility and you both commit to this search for truth. If you charge ahead without that 'willingness check', an in-depth Socratic dialogue can end up feeling more like a police interrogation:

'Do you mind if I ask you a few questions about this?'

'What if we look at this issue together?'

'Do you fancy taking a look at this idea from every angle?'

Opening gambits like these ensure that your conversation partner knows what's coming (i.e. probing, critical questions). They are aware that this is going to be more challenging than a friendly chat and can decide for themselves whether or not to participate.

That last point is essential: the other person has to feel they have the opportunity to say 'no' to your proposal for critical questioning. No matter how much you want to, no matter how convinced you are that the other person stands to benefit, no matter how curious you are about the truths waiting to be unlocked by your questions, without a commitment from the other person, any discussion you attempt will be a pointless exercise and you are more likely to encounter resistance than gain anything more valuable.

This explicit commitment also has the advantage of serving as a reference point later in the conversation: if things start to get a little fraught or you feel you're beginning to tread into dangerous territory, you can reassess whether or not the commitment is still there on both sides. This leaves the other person free to halt the conversation at any time, and you can also check by asking them if they still want to continue. Sometimes a partner simply won't want to take the conversation as far as you do … Such is life.

Socrates and Protagoras

In his article 'The Socratic dialogue as a tool for team-reflection', philosopher Hans Bolten gives us a good example of how Socrates asked his conversation partner for their commitment. He explains how Socrates discusses the topic of virtue with Protagoras, a sophist. A sophist was someone who travelled from town to town to teach, to give instructions, often to young men from rich families with an interest in a career in politics. This paid well, and since Socrates had a friend who was interested in the teachings of Protagoras and would have to pay a lot of money, Socrates is curious as to what Protagoras has to offer.

'Needless to say, Protagoras has his sales pitch ready,' Bolten writes in his article. 'He teaches a young man "prudence in affairs private as well as public […] to order his own house in the best manner, and […] to speak and act for the best in the affairs of the state".'[2]

Bolten then describes how Protagoras goes on to talk about 'political virtue, which proceeds only by way of justice and wisdom':[3]

'Then,' says Socrates, 'you do indeed possess a noble art, if there is no mistake about this' and goes on to express serious doubts as to whether it's possible for Protagoras to possess it at all! After all, Socrates says, even 'the best and wisest of our citizens' have not been able to teach virtue to their children. But, if Protagoras thinks otherwise, then I am willing to concede he might be mistaken.' In short, Socrates invites Protagoras to join him in examining this issue.

SOCRATES: Now I [...] having these examples before me, am inclined to think that virtue cannot be taught. But then again, when I listen to your words, I am disposed to waver; and I believe that there must be something in what you say, because I know that you have great experience, and learning, and invention. And I wish that you would, if possible, show me a little more clearly that virtue can be taught. Will you be so good?
PROTAGORAS: That I will, Socrates, and gladly.[4]

'This immediately highlights two characteristics of Socrates's approach to philosophising,' Bolten explains. First: by asking 'can virtue be taught or not?' Socrates establishes a single, very clear question. Second: he extends an open invitation to Protagoras to participate in this enquiry, and Protagoras accepts this invitation. 'Protagoras is not dragged into this inquiry against his will,' Bolten writes. This invitation may seem unimportant, but it is not to be underestimated:

It may seem like a fairly obvious move to 'just check' whether Protagoras is open to investigating the issue with him and to make sure he is invested enough in their shared quest – but there's more to it than that. The importance of this invitation can hardly be overestimated. Throughout the conversation that follows, Socrates keeps returning to Protagoras's willingness or unwillingness to pull his weight in their joint endeavour. On more than one occasion he emphasises that it's not in the least necessary or self-evident for them to make this inquiry together – both parties are equally free to end the conversation at any time. And as long as neither of them leave, they're not having the conversation at Socrates's insistence, but because they both want to.[5]

Exercise: ask permission for a philosophical enquiry

The next time you hear someone say something interesting, a point that you'd like to explore, why not pop the question: 'Do you fancy taking a closer look at this?' or 'We could take a philosophical look at this together – are you up for it?' Of course, find words that feel natural to you. It doesn't matter whether or not you dive in right then and there. Perhaps the other person doesn't have the time, but would be happy to give it a go later. The main thing is to get used to inviting someone to commit to an in-depth conversation.

CONDITION FOUR

Slow things down

To ask really good questions and explore the answers, you need to slow things down a little. Accept the idea that a genuine dialogue takes time, attention and discipline. A good dialogue – one where you move forward step by step, listening to arguments along the way, tuning in to what's being said both explicitly and between the lines – doesn't stand a chance at our normal speed of conversation. It requires the same commitment and concentration as solving a complex puzzle, doing calligraphy or threading a fine needle with woolly gloves on. It's not something we're all that familiar with, so it's bound to take some getting used to at first. Genuine dialogue needs slow thinking and slow speaking, and those are skills that we need to train.

Take the time it takes, so it takes less time

I once attended a lecture given by an honest-to-goodness cowboy. He didn't disappoint: tough-guy demeanour, leather boots, checked shirt and Stetson. His specialism was loading trailers. If you ever want to tow a reluctant horse in a trailer behind your car, he's your man. Transporting a horse in a trailer is a little like carrying a bird around in a handbag. Horses are born to charge across wide-open plains, and so they're claustrophobic by nature. The fact that we get them to stand in a narrow box on wheels at all is a miracle.

A surprising number of horse owners never think to train their horse to handle a trailer. When it's time to take them to the vet or to a competition, they drive up at the last minute and expect the horse to trot right in. The clock is ticking, nerves are on edge and it all needs to happen in a hurry. The result? A horse up on its hind legs or straining every sinew in a tug-of-war with its owner – in short, the last thing you want! How much easier would it have been if, with a little planning one quiet afternoon, they'd thought, 'Let's just see if I can get the horse to walk into the trailer. No pressure, if it doesn't work out.' If they had, the horse would very likely have been in its trailer in no time at all. As the cowboy said during his talk, the lesson here is, 'Take the time it takes, so it takes less time.'

I think the same applies to a good conversation. You need to slow down to get there quicker. In the longer term, adopting easy-going intention – the idea of taking all the time and space you need in order to have a good dialogue – will be much more rewarding than a seemingly super-efficient but ultimately rushed encounter.

Exercise: easy does it

For this exercise it's useful to ask someone to practise with you, so that you can both experience what slowing down a conversation can do for you. Ask a nice, juicy, stimulating question. When your conversation partner replies, ask another question, and go on repeating this process. There's only one rule: before every question and before every answer, you both have to be quiet for twenty seconds. Of course you are free to spend those twenty seconds biting your tongue, raring to have your say, but why would you? Instead use the time to mull over the question the other person has asked or the answer they have given. Make a conscious effort to 'stick with the question' or 'stick with the idea'. Observe what you're thinking. When the twenty seconds are up, ask your next question or give your next answer, but do it calmly. After about ten minutes you can swap roles, and of course it's worth having a chat about the experience once you're finished: what benefits, if any, did your delaying tactics give you?

Here are a few questions to get you started:

- What would you do differently tomorrow if money was no object?
- How do you know you own something?
- What should you not be allowed to complain about?
- Who shouldn't you have to take seriously?
- Why do people always want to be right?

I once gave a talk at a big Dutch bank about three lessons we can learn from Socrates. The participants were all business leaders, accustomed to making snap decisions, to juggling contacts and priorities all day long: a roomful of keen minds that never stopped racing. I told them a thing or two about developing a Socratic attitude and wanted them to experience a few of the principles involved. I got them to do the above exercise – asking a juicy question and leaving a twenty-second space before they responded – and, from my vantage point onstage, it was a treat to see what happened: their faces began to relax, I could see them thinking more about their answers, and the connection between questioner and respondent began to grow. You could feel the energy in the room change.

CONDITION FIVE

Tolerate frustration

A conversation that's slow, that requires attention and discipline and involves asking critical questions that confront the other person with their own, sometimes deficient arguments and opinions invariably comes with a helping of frustration – on both sides. At times the other person may become offended when their views (and therefore aspects of their identity) are questioned. They may also find it hard to contain their impatience with a conversation that's unfolding at a slower pace than normal, and feel frustrated by what they experience as your lack of emotion as you focus on collaborative thinking.

These feelings are all part of the process. Dialogue training is like going to the gym: your thinking muscles need time to adapt. At first the aches and pains are all that you notice. It's only after a while that you feel yourself getting stronger. I accept that my conversation partner will sometimes blame me for their conversational aches and pains, just as I sometimes lie there on my mat inwardly cursing my gym instructor. But bear with it. It's nothing personal. Above all, be aware that frustration is a good sign. This is *elenchus* and it's a sign that some real effort is being put in, something is shifting, someone's thinking is being stretched. The gym instructor doesn't take our groaning and dirty looks personally, either. Inwardly they're thinking, 'That's more like it. Good workout!'

If anything, frustration is fuel for your exploration. It tells you something about the other person's thinking patterns. The question 'What's making you feel frustrated right now?' has led to many an insight during workshops and consultations. Some people become annoyed when it turns out that their argument isn't nearly as strong as they thought it was, while others are frustrated by their own stubbornness and the fact that they really don't want to change their point of view. First and foremost, frustration is a sign that a person has become stuck in their own mode of thinking. Your task, as a budding practical philosopher, is to show them where they're stuck and to help them think their way out of their rut.

Exercise: tolerate frustration

Have a conversation that brings together everything you've picked up so far: ask permission to hold an in-depth discussion, listen purely and attentively to the language being used, ask follow-up questions, confront and check in with your conversation partner, where necessary, and explore your chosen topic together. As soon as you sense the other person becoming frustrated, check in with yourself quickly first: stay calm and don't take their frustration personally – it honestly isn't personal – even if they react by putting the blame on you. And then you have a choice: do you want to stick to your Socratic 'what-exactly-do-you-mean?' attitude, or do you want to switch up your approach, acknowledge their frustration and ask them what they think is happening? 'I couldn't help but notice that you sighed just now. What does that mean?' Or 'You look annoyed. What's bothering you?'

With any luck, Part Three has left you familiar with the fundamental Socratic conditions for asking questions. Everything starts with listening, pure and simple. Remember to take language seriously, ask permission to question the other person and check in with them if things start to get a little tense. The key is to slow things down and learn to better sit with the feelings of frustration – the other person's as well as your own – that can arise as a result of a meaningful and exploratory Socratic discussion.

PART FOUR

Questioning skills: techniques, tips and pitfalls

Again, and as always,
and as seen above
there are no questions more urgent
than naive questions.

Wisława Szymborska, 'The Turn of the Century'[1]

A WHOLE BOOK ABOUT asking questions and *now* we get to the practical tips and tricks? You might ask, 'Why the wait? What's wrong with supplying a neat list of fail-safe questioning techniques up front?' The answer is simple: that's not how this works. There is no strict manual or fail-safe user's guide to asking the right questions. Of course there are countless checklists and handbooks you can flip through, but if there's no foundation in place – that is, your Socratic attitude and basic conditions – you can still miss the mark by a country mile. There you stand with your list of Socratic questions for beginners, only to forge ahead in 'what-do-I-think?' mode and barely scratch the surface in your search for shared wisdom. That's why the practical questioning tips and tricks don't appear until Part Four. Here come the techniques that always work, but only when coupled with a solid foundation: your Socratic questioning attitude.

A GUIDE TO ASKING SOCRATIC QUESTIONS: UPS AND DOWNS

An opinion is an end point. If I come out with a statement like 'I think Mark is a good father', you have no idea what I'm basing that opinion on. Even as I speak the words, there's every chance I don't really know myself. All I know is that I think Mark is a good father. But there are a ton of reasons why I might think this way and, unless you ask me to explain it, my notion of 'good fatherhood' is anyone's guess. Mark might be protective or give his kids a lot of freedom. He might ask a lot of his children or nothing at all. Until you ask me, your assessment of my statement will be based on your own ideas about what makes a good father. And they may well be completely different from my own.

To get to grips with the hidden arguments that underlie a judgement, you need good questions. The key to asking Socratic questions is, of course, a Socratic attitude, but Socratic questions are always attached to a concrete example. An actual event, statement or action – in this instance, an example of something I consider to be good fatherhood. Although juggling abstract concepts can be fun for a while, without a concrete example, a conversation based around them can soon become vague and difficult to follow.

To keep a dialogue manageable, philosopher Hans Bolten has developed a handy structure: he subdivides Socratic enquiry into 'upward' and 'downward' questions. Upward questions tend towards the abstract, while downward questions are designed to root around in the specifics of the concrete situation.

Dividing the world into up and down for a while can be a big help when it comes to pursuing a consistent line of Socratic questioning. First, we have the observable facts – reality unfolding before our very eyes, a bit like a movie. Something happens and we register that occurrence with one or more of our senses. This is the 'down' zone: everyday life, concrete reality. Someone says or does something and we hear or see it. More often than not, we'll also have a few thoughts about it, too. So far, so good. But when we start talking about that reality and what we think of it, things become more complicated. We come out with a statement, we make an assertion. This is an important moment, because without an assertion and an argument, there would be precious little to question.

For example, Anja might say, 'Thea's a true friend.' Or 'That guy Jeremy is a solid worker.' Behind these simple assertions lies a world of beliefs, presuppositions, values and even notions of human nature. These belong to the 'up' zone in our 'up/down' analysis: they are the abstract concepts and labels we so often attach to the reality of 'being'. The notions 'true friend' and 'solid worker' are examples of these abstract concepts. So too are things like honesty, justice, friendship, solidarity, racism, openness, courage and cooperation.

This 'up/down' view leaves us with concrete reality 'below', and abstract concepts (norms, values, beliefs, humanity and world view) 'above'. The diagram on the next page presents this in greater detail.

If you keep this up/down distinction clearly in mind, you can always head in two directions with your questions. You can ask about the facts of the situation and, in the same conversation, you can ask about the relevant values and views of human nature. Downward questions are factual: designed to extract information concerning the nuts and bolts of the situation. What does Jeremy actually do that makes him such a solid worker? What is it about Thea that makes Anja value her as a friend? The answer to a downward question will provide concrete evidence to back up the initial statement. The answer might be something like 'Jeremy is a solid worker because he completes his assignments on time and keeps his appointments.' Or 'Thea is a true friend, because she really listens to what I have to say and sometimes helps me pick up the kids from school.'

By asking an upward question, you can then address the arguments and presuppositions behind that statement: 'Why

THINKING

Abstract concepts, beliefs, ideas about human nature, moral
principles (e.g. honesty, justice, courage, being a good
mother or a good colleague)

Asking upwards:

- What does X have to do with Y?
- Why is that?
- What do you mean by 'X'?

STATEMENT – assertion

I think that . . .
I hope that . . .
I believe that . . .
I expect that . . .

Asking downwards:

- When did this happen?
- What exactly did he say?
- What did you do next?
- What happened from there?

BEING

Concrete reality:
Facts, actions, events, statements
Perceptible, identifiable
(e.g. There were seven people at the meeting.
It was raining. He said, 'Don't be so stupid.'
She took out a dark-green handkerchief.)[2]

is someone who really listens a true friend?' One possible
answer is 'Because it shows that they are genuinely interested
in other people.' That in turn would tell us that Anja believes
it's important for friends to show an interest in one another.
That may seem obvious, but someone else might easily take
a very different view of what friendship entails.

The case of the good mother

A while back, I gave the following assignment to the students on my 'Philosophy in Everyday Life' course. First, I sketched a scenario for them. A girl who lives on an island wants to visit her boyfriend on the mainland. There's a storm and the ferry is cancelled. The only boatman on the island is willing to take the girl to the mainland, but only if she sleeps with him first. The girl goes to her mother for advice. Her mother says the decision is entirely up to her.

Then I asked my students, 'Is she a good mother?'

Two of my students, Ryan and Marcel, each had a different answer. Marcel didn't think she was a good mother, while Ryan disagreed. Initially neither of them was really able to explain why they felt that way. My conversation with Marcel went like this:

> MARCEL: I don't think she's a good mother. I honestly think what she did is plain wrong.
> ELKE: What exactly did she do that you think is wrong? [downward question]
> MARCEL: She literally says, 'You should make up your own mind.' She just abandoned her daughter to her fate.
> ELKE: What did the mother do that makes you say she abandoned her daughter to her fate? [another downward question]

MARCEL: She didn't give her daughter any advice at all. She only said, 'Honey, it is your choice to make.' She didn't try to protect her from the boatman!

ELKE: So being a good mother is related to protection? [upward question]

MARCEL: Yes, I think it is. A good mother would have protected her daughter from harm and given her advice when she asked for it.

Ryan still wasn't convinced and thought the mother in the story was a good mother. My exchange with Ryan went something like this:

RYAN: I don't share Marcel's view at all. To me, she sounds like a good mother.

ELKE: What does she do, exactly, that makes her a good mother? [downward question]

RYAN: She doesn't give advice. That's the whole point! She literally says, 'It is your choice to make.'

ELKE: What's good about the mother not giving her daughter advice? [upward question]

RYAN: When you don't give someone advice, they have to rely on their own ideas, their own thoughts. You give them responsibility. That is what this mother does.

ELKE: So for you, being a good mother has something to do with letting your child take responsibility for their own actions? [upward question]

RYAN: Exactly!

Two simple conversations that demonstrate the need to question someone to find out why they're saying what they're saying. Before answering these questions, Ryan and Marcel themselves didn't really know what they thought about motherhood. If I had bypassed this concrete example and asked them a relatively abstract question like 'What constitutes a good mother?' they would probably have agreed on something much more vague.

Broad labels and capacious concepts such as 'motherhood', 'responsibility' and 'freedom' only become meaningful when you actually attach them to something concrete. In this case to a simple story about a girl who wants to go and see her boyfriend. In our day-to-day lives we pass judgement on the stuff of everyday life and rarely scrutinise our general concepts and sweeping definitions.

After this conversation Marcel said, 'Goodness, I can see how having a conversation like that with someone else could help you discover that neither of you really knows what the other person stands for or thinks is important. And without it, you could spend ages locked in a needless disagreement.'

First down, then up

For a good Socratic conversation, you want to start by getting the facts straight. What exactly happened? Who was involved and how did the situation unfold? First of all, that means fact-finding: asking questions that drill down into the specifics. The aim is to have a kind of YouTube clip of the event in your mind, with nothing blocked or pixelated. You want a clear view of what took place, without having to rely on your imagination to fill in parts of the action. The other person will probably want to take things up to the abstract level faster than you do, but that's okay. Just keep plugging away with your factual questions until you know exactly what happened. Once you have that clear in your own mind, you can change direction and start asking upward questions.

If you're not sure which direction to take with your questions, it's better to go down instead of up. There's a good reason for this: your respondent will often tend towards thinking and talking at a relatively abstract level, in any case. If you head upwards from there, you can easily lose the thread and drift off the point. If you want to bring focus and depth to your conversation, it makes sense to keep bringing the other person back to the real-world example.

Once you do that, application to your everyday life is not all that hard to imagine – for example, try listening closely to a radio or TV interview or an episode of a podcast. Listen carefully to the questions being asked and decide whether the direction is up or down. Is this a question aimed at getting to grips with the facts and what actually happened (downward)? Or is it focused more on opinions, values, presuppositions or ideas of what people are, or should be, like (upward)? A spot of analytical eavesdropping can really cement your grasp of question structure and enable you to apply it more easily in your own conversations.

Exercise: try the 'down then up' technique

Pay close attention when someone makes a statement. For example, when they comment on something that happened to them or talk about 'the way things are'. Try questioning them on that statement: first down, and then up. For instance, someone might say, 'I was at the PTA meeting this evening, and Patrick – you know, Martha's dad – started going on about renovating the school playground for the umpteenth time. It was so condescending. I mean, the headmaster was sitting right there!'

Your downward questions might be:

- What exactly did Patrick say?
- What are the renovations to the playground?
- Who else was at the meeting?
- What did the others say?

Upward questions might include:

- What was condescending about Patrick's comments?
- Is it wrong to be condescending?
- Is Patrick not allowed to be condescending?

QUESTIONS THAT REACH THE CRITICAL POINT

In the Socratic method you keep asking questions until you reach the critical point: the moment on which everything hinges. Imagine: you're standing at the supermarket checkout and someone jumps the queue. It makes you angry. Telling someone about an incident like that later, you often descend into a jumble of words and the whole story is framed by your anger. Yet if you look closely, there's one specific point at which the anger arises. It wasn't there throughout the experience – it appeared. You can almost pinpoint that moment. *That's* when the anger started.

Perhaps it was something the queue-jumper said, or the moment his trolley bumped into yours. Perhaps it was the moment he pretended not to see you and slipped into the line ahead of you. Perhaps your anger began with the thought, 'What does he think he's doing?' By going in search of that critical point, you get to the heart of someone's story. And once you reach it, you can go on asking about the reasons behind their anger, sadness, frustration, perception, opinion or point of view.

Asking until you reach the critical point means asking downward questions. You're asking for a thorough, blow-by-blow account of the scene: what exactly went on, who was there, what was said. Once you have that footage and a clear understanding of what happened, you can continue by asking upward questions. What does the person make of these facts and events? That will result in a core assertion: 'Then [at the critical point] … I did/thought/felt … because …'

From here, you can continue to probe by asking further questions. For example: 'When the man said, "I've just got the one item, mate" and pushed in, I was angry because it's rude to assume it's okay to jump the queue without even waiting for a reply.'

This core assertion brings together all kinds of aspects that you can follow up on by asking upward questions. What constitutes rudeness? Why should you wait for a reply? Did the man have reasons for doing what he did? And so on. By first shining a light on the critical point and identifying the core assertion, you can then address the specific event as it happened and bring more sharpness and depth to your conversation.

The case of the lazy daughter

During a training course on Socratic questioning, Nadia contributed the following assertion: my daughter is terribly lazy. Arnold was given the task of questioning Nadia and homing in on the critical point. This meant eliciting a concrete example from Nadia and then obtaining the clearest possible picture of this example. That involved drilling down with his questions until he could see the scene Nadia had described, like a movie, in his mind's eye.

NADIA: My daughter Hannah is terribly lazy. I came home yesterday to find her lounging on the couch, mucking about on her smartphone, with the TV on full blast. Even though she's got a ton of homework to do and her exams are next week.

ARNOLD: What time did you get home?

NADIA: After school, around 4.30.

ARNOLD: Where were you when you saw her lounging in front of the TV?

NADIA: I got home from work at 4.30 with a bag of groceries. The door to the living room was open. I looked in on my way to the kitchen and that's when I saw her.

ARNOLD: Did you say anything to each other?

NADIA: I certainly did. I saw her lounging there and said, 'Sitting comfortably?' She gave her usual adolescent 'Hm'. And then I said, 'Don't you have homework or revision to do?'

ARNOLD: And then?

NADIA: Then she just sighed and rolled her eyes, and I took the groceries into the kitchen.

In a Socratic discussion, you often write down the example, so the whole group can follow along. Writing things down also enables the person telling the story to see if they've skipped anything. You can write the story exactly as told, but a summary is often enough.

> ARNOLD: So if I understand you correctly, it went like this. You come home and when you stop at the living-room door, you see your daughter lounging on the couch, mucking about on her smartphone, with the TV on full blast. You say, 'Sitting comfortably?' and she answers, 'Hm.' You ask, 'Don't you have homework to do?' and she sighs and rolls her eyes. Then you take the groceries into the kitchen.

Note that Arnold deliberately repeats Nadia's exact words as much as possible, as he goes over what she's told him so far. He tries not to paraphrase or to summarise in his own words, and he is careful not to introduce new ideas, words or concepts. Instead he sticks as closely as possible to exactly what Nadia told him. This is as it should be, and is a technique we'll return to in Part Five, when we discuss good follow-up questions in more detail. Arnold checks that Nadia agrees with his summary and then, once the scenario is clear and the scene looks roughly the same for both parties, he pursues his line of questioning in search of the critical point.

> ARNOLD: At what moment did you think your daughter was lazy?

NADIA: Right away. As soon as I looked into the living room and saw her. I half-expected her to be lounging around like that and, sure enough …

ARNOLD: So at what point did you think what exactly?

NADIA: When I stopped in the doorway and saw her lounging on the couch with her smartphone and the TV on, I thought: 'There she is, being lazy again!'

From this critical moment, Arnold can start to direct his questions upwards. He now knows that, in Nadia's mind, 'lounging on the couch with your smartphone in front of the TV' equates to 'being lazy'. What he still doesn't know is why she thinks this. The aim at this point is to work together to examine what kinds of judgements, presuppositions and ideas about human nature are woven into Nadia's way of thinking.

ARNOLD: What does lounging on the couch with your smartphone and watching TV have to do with 'being lazy'?

NADIA: Well, you're not doing anything useful. You're doing nothing. Just taking up space.

ARNOLD: Is someone who isn't doing anything useful automatically lazy?

NADIA: Well, no, not necessarily. You can do something that's not useful without being lazy, of course.

ARNOLD: Was Hannah doing anything useful when you looked in on her?

NADIA: No. Well, I don't know. I don't think so. I don't really know what she was doing on her smartphone. I didn't ask.

ARNOLD: So how does what she was doing relate to being lazy?

NADIA: I'm not exactly sure any more. That's just how I see it.

In the above dialogue, you can see how Arnold starts with downward questions, then switches upwards, and then moves downwards again. He persists in his questions when Nadia doesn't really give a clear answer, and Nadia in turn sees her strongly held opinion start to crumble. It's at this point that *elenchus* and *aporia* put in an appearance. By the end of their exchange, Nadia has lost the courage of her convictions. By now, it has become crystal-clear that 'being lazy' is more a factor in Nadia's perception than it is in Hannah's behaviour. When Nadia is asked to be exact about her evidence, it turns out she doesn't have much concrete evidence at all, other than a vague sense of 'laziness' somehow being opposed to 'usefulness'.

Exercise: moving upwards from the critical point

For this exercise, find someone who wants to practise with you and who knows that they are going to be Socratically questioned. Ask them to think of an event that had an emotional impact on them. For example, a situation that involved irritation, anger or a harsh judgement. Then ask questions about that event from every angle until you have the scene clear in your head. You can take notes or write a summary – whatever works best for you. Then home in on the critical point. 'At what point did your anger ignite?' 'At what point did you think "What a jerk!"?' Try to pinpoint that moment as precisely as possible, to the second. Then ask upward questions like: 'What does this behaviour have to do with being a jerk?' and see if you can arrive at a clear assertion: 'Then [at the critical point] ... I did/thought/felt ... because ...' From that moment on, you can ask upward as well as downward questions, with the aim of exploring the other person's thought processes. What judgements or assumptions are shaping their thinking without them even knowing? Play, explore and discover. And, above all, enjoy the ride.

The structure provided by upward and downward questioning will give you a firmer grip on all your conversations, especially ones where you want to work with the other person to get to the bottom of something. Everything you have discovered so far in this book comes together in this process. Naturally you need your questioning Socratic attitude, and it's important to have the other person's permission before you start questioning them. Remember that you may well encounter the irritation that comes with *elenchus* and *aporia*, and this indicates that there's room for all kinds of new and surprising insights to occur. Don't be afraid to fail, or to ask a vague or stupid question. There's nothing wrong with that. Put on your skates and step out onto the ice: you'll only learn to ask good Socratic questions by trying, falling flat on your face once in a while and getting right back up on your feet.

A RECIPE FOR ASKING GOOD QUESTIONS: PIE IN THE SKY?

Key ingredients for a Socratic attitude
- Take curiosity as your base
- Add a dash of not-knowing
- A teaspoon of naivety
- A pinch of desire for a deeper understanding
- A helping of patience
- Keep your opinions on ice
- Leave your empathy on the shelf
- A generous stretch of time
- An empty head and eyes wide open.

You've developed your Socratic attitude, you know how to create the conditions for a good, in-depth conversation and you've got a firm grip on how to handle upward and downward questions. Does that mean you're ready to roll? Almost! The icing on the cake comes in the shape of a series of highly practical, directly applicable tips for all your questions, regardless of the type of conversation you plan to have. A collection of tips and tricks for asking good questions. What's the deal with closed questions? Are they allowed or not? And what about that most intimidating of questions: why? Should you be asking it or not? How can you make sure someone immediately understands your question without feeling threatened or offended by it? What other question tips are there, and do they always work?

I once gave a workshop on interview techniques to a group of young consultants in the financial sector. There they sat in a circle, looking at me expectantly. I asked them what they already knew about asking good questions. 'You have to ask open questions,' one said. And the whole group nodded in agreement.

It's a view I often encounter: an open question is a good question. Perhaps it's also a view you share. To be frank, I've never understood where that conviction comes from: it's really not very helpful at all. By branding open questions as the only ones worth asking, we sell closed questions short.

When is a question open or closed?

Before you read on, take a moment to ask yourself this question: do you know how to recognise when a question is closed and when it's open?

The answer I usually get when I ask this question at a course or workshop goes something like this: 'You can only answer yes or no to a closed question, but an open question invites a longer answer.' But that's only partly true. A closed question may be designed to elicit a yes-or-no answer, but who said conversation was predictable? I know people who will happily launch into their life story in response to a closed question; and others who, when asked an open question, will venture no further than a simple yes or no. When you define questions in this way, your definition depends on the answer you get and overlooks the structure of the question itself.

A classification based on the structure of the question itself is much neater and easier to use. Open questions start with the words we most readily associate with a question: who, what, where, which, when, how or what for? A closed question always begins with a verb or a conjugation thereof.

But even this doesn't quite cover all the bases. Take the question 'Who is the Queen of England?' Is that an open question or a closed question? By the definition above, it should be open because it starts with 'who'. Even if there appears to be only one answer. But then that's not quite true, either, because a child could easily answer that their mum is the Queen of England. And so it's a different question from the closed variant 'Is Elizabeth II the Queen of England?' To that last, closed question, only one correct answer is possible.[3]

Depending on your purpose, a closed question can sometimes be your most effective tool. If you just want to check something, ask a closed question. Does your conversation partner tend to ramble on a bit? By asking closed questions, you increase the likelihood that their answers will become more concrete and to the point. If the other person comes out with a muddled story that's awash with emotions, then closed questions can help structure the narrative and clear a clouded head. But if someone is reluctant to provide information, closed questions probably aren't going to help matters.

Perhaps more importantly, closed questions can often be the most thought-provoking questions. 'Do you always have to be honest?' 'Does knowledge gained through experience make you an expert?' 'Is it okay to lie to a friend?' 'Is helping always the right thing to do?' When it comes to focusing the mind and thinking about issues that matter, a closed question is often a better opener than a perfectly acceptable open question.

Of course you still need to be careful that your closed question remains a proper question, and that you're not asking a leading question or steering your respondent towards giving a particular answer. But by all means use them! In the right hands, a closed question is just as effective a tool as an open one. Limiting your options by believing that you shouldn't ask closed questions is a real pity and is not the least bit necessary.

Pay attention to the first word of your question

Note the first word of your question. If it's a negative verb, the chances are that your question is leading, or that you are checking a hypothesis or even asking a rhetorical question: 'Didn't that meeting go on for ever?'

It's fine to start a question with a verb, mainly if you want to check specific information. 'Can you see that plane up there?' is an acceptable question if you're about to tell a person something about the aircraft in question and you want to make sure you're both looking at the same object. But when you want to get the other person to supply you with input of their own, the question 'What do you see?' would be more appropriate.

If your question starts with a verb, especially if it's negative, be sure to check very carefully whether it's a question at all and not simply a statement packaged as a question. If the latter is true, don't waste a good question, and simply say what you want to say. If your question starts with a statement, you can be pretty sure that it's not a genuine question but a rhetorical one. 'The reports were supposed to be sent yesterday, right?' 'Dirty clothes belong in the laundry basket, don't they?'

Exercise: recognising open and closed questions

Over the next couple of days, pay attention to the questions people ask. In everyday conversations, in the press, on TV. In each case, try to determine for yourself whether the question is open or closed. Not by checking out the answer, but by sticking to the structure of the question. Once you've got that sorted, switch your focus to the answers the question elicits. Do people respond differently, depending on whether a question is open or closed?

The myth of the 'why' question

Many guides to questioning techniques advise people not to ask why. That's a real shame, because 'why' is one of the most important questions to ask if you want to gain new insights and deepen your understanding. That said, the question 'why' does come with a pocket-sized instruction manual. Sometimes being asked why makes people feel that they are being attacked. After all, we're not used to being questioned on matters that are self-evident to us. Having to explain what you think and why you think it can be rather unsettling, and often people clam up when faced with the question 'why'.

We often interpret a why question as a call to accountability. You can easily feel that you are being asked to defend yourself when you have no cause to. I think it's because we have a tendency to abuse 'why' questions. Instead of being genuinely curious about the other person's motives, we often ask 'why' when we have already drawn our own conclusions and decide to vent our opinion in the form of a question. Instead of saying what's on our mind or what's getting on our nerves, we hit the other person with a question. 'I'm really annoyed with you for not cleaning up when you said you would' becomes 'Why didn't you clean up?' The other person senses immediately that this is not a genuine enquiry, but a criticism packaged as something that resembles a question. All too often there's a punitive edge to our 'why' questions – for instance, 'Why are you working late?' or 'Why do you still eat meat?'

Enquiries like these, according to this book's definition of good questions, are anything but! They come across as critical commentary and hardly ever sound like a sincere question. A good question arises from a sincere and curious attitude, and therefore the so-called questions in the previous paragraph don't measure up in either of these respects. A genuine 'why' question is essential in achieving new insights and new ways of thinking. When you want to bring depth to a conversation, think something through together and challenge someone to look at what's underpinning their own statements, asking a bunch of 'why' questions is a great idea.

We are far too reluctant to ask each other 'why'. It's often out of fear. We're afraid people will think we're out to challenge them or that we'll come across as confrontational. But unless we ask 'why', where are our new insights going to come from? So if you're having a good conversation and the connection between you feels right, don't be afraid to ask a 'why' question when one occurs to you.

However, bearing in mind that defensive reflex, it may still be advisable to tweak the question a little. Unless, of course, the relationship between you and your conversation partner feels warm and safe. Or if, as in a Socratic conversation or a philosophical consultation, you have both agreed beforehand to be offended or take things personally when 'why' questions are invariably asked.

Try reformulating your why questions as follows:

- Why do you still eat meat?
- → What are your reasons for eating meat?

- Why do you think voting should be mandatory?
- → What are your arguments for making voting mandatory?

- Why do you say that?
- → What makes you say that?

There's another pitfall you need to look out for when asking why: a 'why' question can set you on the trail of a single cause or explanation when often there isn't one. In other words, it invites an answer that can easily fall short, because real life is complex and things frequently have more than one cause or reason behind them. For instance, 'Why did the Second World War break out?' Good luck trying to narrow that down to just one!

In cases where you are searching for a single cause, you can be more specific and ask, 'What's the reason that ...', as shown in one of the reformulated examples above. However, if you're hoping to elicit a more complex response, it's better to start your question with 'how'. A question like 'Why did you decide to stop eating meat?' tends to invite a single-explanation answer. But that decision might well have been a process involving a combination of factors. In that case 'How did you arrive at the decision to stop eating meat?' would be the better question to ask.

Exercise: try out variations of 'why'

The next time you find yourself wanting to ask a why question but feel yourself shying away from it, go ahead and ask, but alter the wording. 'Why did you …', for example, might become 'What made you decide to …' See what happens in your conversation: does the other person feel cornered and become defensive? Or do they keep talking and give you a deeper insight into their way of thinking?

The magic phrase that always invites people to say more

A while back I gave my workshop on the art of asking questions to a team of workers at a housing association. I started by asking them to share what they wanted to get out of the workshop. Their answers included 'How do I ask questions that encourage someone to get to the point?', 'What can I ask to get the other person thinking?' and 'How can

I confront a customer with what they have said by asking good questions?'

One participant, Leonora, said, 'I have three children, aged eleven, nine and seven. I'm always asking them how they're getting on at school and things like that, but I barely get more than a 'fine', 'good' or 'yeah, okay' out of them. How can I ask questions that encourage them to share more?'

As well as listening purely and simply, and not sneaking suggestions, solutions or advice into your questions, there's something else you can do to get less talkative types to open up. There's a little phrase that always seems to work. It helps you stick with the other person's viewpoint, without steering or working your own intentions into the situation, and it's as simple as it is effective:

'Tell me …'

The love of my life has a talent for complaining. If he doesn't get enough sleep, even if it's only by half an hour, storm clouds start to gather overhead. He's also one of those expressive souls who has no reservations about airing whatever's going on inside his head. In his grouchiest of moods – few and far between, thank goodness! – the result is a furious bout of verbal diarrhoea. He literally grumbles out loud about everything. As someone who likes to solve my own problems without bothering other people, this behaviour can spark considerable irritation in me. My instinct is either to play down his predicament – 'Come on, it's not that bad. You can catch up on your sleep tonight' – or to insist that he stop being such a baby about things. As you might expect, neither option really works, and often I succeed only in fanning the flames of his discontent. The result? Even more grouching! Because now his lack of sleep has been compounded by a nagging partner who can't even let him have a good moan once in a while.

What *does* work is the magic 'tell me' phrase. Now whenever my partner is in full-on grouch mode ('Why can I never find anything in this shoebox of a kitchen? Nothing's where it's supposed to be. It drives me mad') I toss in a simple 'What's up? Tell me' and it honestly works miracles. After another spot of grumbling in response, I ask if there's anything I can do to help and, before you know it, the storm has passed.

'Tell me' is like a valve. Flip it open and all those bottled-up emotions, suppressed feelings and the litany of complaints that goes with them are better able to flow out and ebb away.

It gives you the inside story about what's on the other person's mind and a glimpse into their way of thinking. What you do next, of course, depends on how your relationship works and how you *want* it to work. If you sense that it might be helpful to get to the root of something and you want to dig a little deeper, you can try slipping into questioning mode. If things are more or less okay as they are, after using 'tell me', you can simply go about your business.

Exercise: 'Tell me ...'

The next time someone starts moaning when you are around, throw a genuinely interested 'tell me' into the conversation. Keep to yourself things like advice, questions and your desire to help, and make 'Hey, tell me! What happened?' your opening gambit. Notice how the other person responds to your invitation. How does it affect your interaction with them?

QUESTION PITFALLS AND CATEGORIES

Without knowing, we tumble into at least a hundred question pitfalls every day. These are often very simple to sort out – ones you can easily skirt around in future, as soon as your eyes have been opened. And then there are some that you continue to fall into without even realising it. Knowing the pitfalls and the different categories of questions, and learning how to recognise them when they crop up in everyday conversation, can help you have better and more rewarding conversations.

Anyone for tennis?

Asking good questions is like a game of tennis: a player hits a well-aimed shot across the net and waits for the other player to return the ball. Once you've hit the ball, there's no point in firing three more balls at your opponent for good measure. Or in closing your eyes when you swing, so that you have no idea where the ball is going to land. And there's certainly no point in chasing after the ball you've just hit so that you can try to adjust its trajectory in mid-flight. Nor is there any point in standing next to your opponent, whispering instructions on how they should hit the ball in return. Or in juggling three tennis balls while your opponent is waiting for you to play on. Or in giving your opponent a good telling-off if they don't hit the shot you expected them to.

Yet we do exactly that, with alarming regularity, when we ask questions in our everyday lives. Instead of formulating a question, asking it and waiting attentively for the other person to answer, we do anything but. We fire even more questions at them, or explain our question – turning it into more of a monologue or a comment in the process – or go on rambling for so long that we not only introduce distractions from whatever question we just asked, but also drain that question of its clarity and power.

Why ask a question when you want to make a point?

Your first check should be: do I want to ask something or make a point? As you now know, many of our questions aren't questions at all. They are messages in disguise. A statement with a question mark attached. If you have something to say, then say it; don't turn it into a question. That will only create interference and cause hassle. Slow down, take a moment and if you want to make a point, make sure it's a statement that comes out of your mouth, not a question. Tell a story, present your opinion, enter into an argument. But don't come out with a question that isn't really a question at all.

To return to our tennis metaphor, asking a question when you want to make a point is like whacking a tennis ball over the net and then following it up with a baseball, a basketball and a football at lightning speed. Things become very confused. What game are you playing? What are the rules? Whose turn is it and how is the other person supposed to respond?

We often ask questions without really knowing what we want to do with them. We start chatting away and, before we know it, a question has popped out. That question is often unclear and may not even be recognisable as a question. We juggle multiple tennis balls, hit one over every now and then, not necessarily in the right direction, and then chuck another one after it because … well, why the hell not?

So ask yourself first: what's the aim of my question? What sort of category does it fall under? There are several things you can do with a question: check the facts, confront, bring depth to the conversation, set a challenge. If you want to get the facts straight, your question will probably begin with 'who', 'what', 'where', 'how' or 'when'. If you want to dig deeper and elicit an argument or a reason from your conversation partner, you usually ask 'why', 'what's the reason that' or 'how did you decide to'. If you want your question to confront, you can present the other person with their own words. Later on, we will explore how you can ask questions that confront people and get them thinking. If you can't think of an aim for your question, it's worth wondering whether you should open your mouth at all and, if you do, whether it should be a question or a statement that comes out.

Category One: Loser questions

This is a lovely category of questions, because they become so obvious and funny when you start to recognise them in yourself and others. Loser questions are ones that imply the recipient is a loser, so obviously that you might as well stick the word 'loser' on the end of the question. These are not sincere questions at all, but comments packaged as questions. Often you might already know the answer and are just asking it to make an impact. Intonation has a lot to do with whether a question contains a silent loser or not.

'Haven't you sent that report yet [loser]?'
'Didn't I just ask you to take the bins out [loser]?'
'Are you late again [loser]?'
'Did you accidentally "reply all" to that email [loser]?'

You've smashed a ball straight at your tennis partner, giving them no chance at all to hit it back. Oh yeah, and you smashed them over their head with their own racket while you're at it.

Category Two: But questions

A subtle but common question pitfall is the 'but question'. That little word 'but' can all too easily sneak in at the start of a question. It may seem like an innocent little filler, but it often betrays what the questioner really thinks about something. It can happen so subtly that we don't really notice it ourselves, but it sends a clear message to the other person. The effect is clearest in combination with a negative: 'But don't you think Maya should have responded differently?' or 'But don't you think the layout of the report needs changing?'

Even without a negative, 'but' makes a subtle difference to a question: 'But can we go to the pool first?' is a different question from 'Can we go to the pool first?' – just as asking, 'But why did you ask Marian?' is different from asking, 'Why did you ask Marian?'

The underlying message of a but question is: I already have an opinion on this, but I'm not coming out with it directly. In other words: 'I'd like to go to the pool first' and 'I don't think you should have asked Marian.'

Category Three: Cocktail questions

Here, a ball! And here's another one! Oh, and I forgot this one! And this one's even better, I'll wallop that across too! Now which one do you want to hit back? No, not that one! That one won't get us anywhere!

We're so good at cocktail questions. We start a question, then come up with a better version, so we ask that too. And sometimes another and another until they are all jumbled together. We create a cocktail of questions that sends the other person's head spinning as they try to work out which one to answer and in what order.

The result is often a vague account or a half-baked answer. As often as not, the other person will just start talking, with no idea of where their words are heading. It's a pity, because by asking several questions at once, you hardly ever get the in-depth conversation you're looking for. Make sure you ask one question, and leave it at that. When you do, the other person will have a clear idea of what they are replying to and – all being well – will give an answer that's fit for purpose. The result is a well-defined exchange, without interference: a response that gives you solid information as the basis for further questions.

Now that you know this, keep your eyes and ears peeled for cocktail questions when you observe and listen to conversations and interviews. What effect does this type of question have on the other person? And on the conversation itself?

Category Four: Vague questions

How often have you been asked a question that leaves you thinking, 'What on earth are they getting at?' A vague question that has you wondering what the person who asked it actually means.

My partner had a habit of waking up on a Sunday morning and asking, 'Is it late?' A vague question that left me to determine what 'late' was. The first time I answered 'yes'. It was 10 a.m., which didn't strike me as especially early, so I decided to label it as late. When he asked me what the time was and I told him it was 10 a.m., he just laughed and said, 'Oh, but that's early!'

With this in mind, make it clear exactly what information you're looking for when you ask a question. Ask an unambiguous question – one that doesn't leave the other person floundering around for what you mean by a certain idea or concept.

So not:

- Is that tower high?
- Was the lasagne tasty?
- Was he fat or thin?

But instead:

- How high is that tower?
- How did the lasagne taste?
- What size was he?

Category Five: The unwarranted either/or question

Do you want peanut butter or jam? There's nothing wrong with asking a question with two options. When you're pushed for time or want to come to a quick decision with someone else, these kinds of questions can be rather helpful, as they simplify the choice to only two options. They are especially useful when the other person is a child who you're making lunch for, and you need to know right away which of the two sandwiches they want to eat. The trouble comes when we choose questions that encourage people to limit their answers to those two options, when in fact there are more:

Do you want to meet today or tomorrow?
- The day after tomorrow or next week might also be an option.

Are you a vegetarian or do you eat meat?
- Again, this is not a black-or-white question. Perhaps you're vegan or pescatarian.

Do you want to go left or right here?
- Straight ahead or back the way you came might be options, too.

When faced with questions like these, we quickly assume that the person asking them has thought things through beforehand and that there really are only two options. But take a closer look at the question and the options on offer, and in fact that's rarely true. It's a bit of a lazy question: you present someone with two options you happen to have come up with yourself, but often there are more. In that case, why not make it an open question? 'What do you want on your sandwich?' 'When do you want to meet?' 'Which direction do you think we should take?'

Category Six: The half-baked question

Many of the questions we ask are only half-finished. It's like serving up a half-baked apple pie. It's hardly recognisable as apple pie and you're not exactly sure what it is you're tasting or what you're supposed to respond to. It can be the same with questions: while a self-contained question is clear, complete and to the point, a half-baked question doesn't stand up on its own or invite a clear response.

If someone comes out with a remark like 'Bram was up to his old tricks again', it may seem perfectly natural to ask 'What do you mean?' This leaves the other person to conclude that you want to know what they mean by their remark about Bram. But as a question, 'What do you mean?' isn't fully formed, as it's not at all clear what part of their statement it's referring to. A piece of the question is missing: 'What do you mean by …?' In this case, 'What do you mean by "old tricks"?'

In the example with Bram, there's probably not that much at stake, but in a more complex situation, things can get trickier:

> So I was walking along the street with Anna and we ran into this guy … you'd know him if you saw him. He was sitting on a bench and he had a pram next to him. He looked up and started yelling at the top of his lungs. It was really odd. We didn't know how to react.

Here again, 'What do you mean?' might feel like a natural question to ask. But it's far from clear whether you're referring to the man, to Anna, to what the man shouted or who he was shouting at – never mind what the pram had to do with any of it. A self-contained question is complete, clear, straightforward and easy to answer. It leaves no room for doubt about the information requested. For example, you might ask: Who's Anna again? Which man do you mean? What exactly did he shout? Who was he shouting at? Why did you think it was really odd?

By being more specific, you stick close to the other person's experience. Your question is focused and you get exactly the information you want.

We're at the end of Part Four, and hopefully you're now familiar with a wide range of questioning skills: the theory behind upward and downward questions; what the critical point is and how to ask follow-up questions in order to arrive at new insights; the common question pitfalls and how to avoid them. In Part Five, the final section, we will take an even closer look at how we question, and will learn how to keep an in-depth conversation going strong.

PART FIVE

From questions to conversation

A broad view expands your thinking.

Loesje[1] ◆

YOU'VE WORKED ON your Socratic attitude and honed your listening skills. You've adopted an open and curious outlook. You've learned how to avoid question pitfalls and apply useful techniques. The moment arrives: you take everything you've learned and pour it into asking a good question. But then what? How do you move from a single question into the flow of an in-depth conversation?

PLAYING DOMINOES

A good conversation with a natural ebb and flow between questions and answers is a bit like an old-fashioned game of dominoes. You lay your dominoes based on the number of dots at either end of the row: a domino with four dots has to connect with another set of four dots, not three, five or six. Ideally, questions and answers should fit together in much the same way. Yet this is far from always the case. Often we end up trying to match six dots with four, or one dot with five.

For instance, you ask a closed question and someone replies by launching into an endless monologue. Or you ask a well-considered open question, only to be greeted with a yes-or-no answer. People can sometimes spend entire conversations talking on different wavelengths. Perhaps the other person only half-listens to your question, which then triggers an association that's all their own and they run with it. You then get so caught up in their response that you also start associating with what *they* are saying and hardly notice that they haven't really answered your question. It's a pattern that characterises many a conversation – stacking one statement, anecdote or opinion on another – instead of playing dominoes and communicating in questions, answers and reactions that genuinely fit together.

But two monologues do not add up to a dialogue. My friend Pippin once told me about a party he was at: 'It was thrown by my father-in-law and I listened in on him talking to a group of guests, all men his own age. It struck me that all they did was tell each other how well they had arranged things for themselves and their families. Pensions, investments – you name it. No one asked anyone else a question. When one had said their piece, someone else chipped in and went one better with their own success story.'

Having a good conversation is not a skill we're born with or that comes naturally. It's something we have to develop through training and practice.

Check your domino: does it fit?

The easiest way to check your dominoes – to see whether the other person's answer follows on from your question – is to filter out the content for a second and instead check the structure of the question and answer. Does a yes-or-no question actually elicit a yes or a no? When you give someone two choices, do they actually choose one or the other, or do they go off on a vaguely related tangent of their own? If you ask, 'What time is it?', does someone actually tell you the time or do they treat you to something completely different?

If you identify something other than what you asked for – if the dots on the dominoes don't match – then it's time to intervene and restore clarity to the conversation. Simply repeating your question usually works best. It's better than playing the smart alec and pointing out to the other person that they haven't actually answered your question.

Here's an example I heard on an Amsterdam tram the other day:

A: Do you fancy sushi? [yes/no question]
B: I went for sushi the other night. What a palaver! The restaurant was mobbed, and every time they came with

our order there was something missing. The waiters were
rushed off their feet and ran around barking at everyone.

Here, a closed question is met with small talk about the
joys or woes of sushi, and it's clear that the conversational
dominoes don't match up.

Things can become a lot trickier when the topic is more
intimate and the people involved feel more vulnerable. When
there's more at stake, people are all too willing to wriggle
out of difficult questions and reluctant to admit that sometimes they just don't know the answer. For example: Tarik
and Anne are Sam's parents. Sam went on a night out with
Peter. There was some drug-taking involved and things got
out of hand.

ANNE: Do you think we should stop Sam going out with
Peter?
TARIK: I think Peter's a nice enough kid, but the last
night out they had together has got me a bit worried.
Some of what went on has me wondering whether …

Anne asks a yes-or-no question, and Tarik answers by
sharing his thoughts. The result is a conversation, but one
that skates across the surface. In Tarik's jumble of words,
his final answer remains unclear.

If you want depth, clarity and a sharper focus, answer
the question first and then go on to share your arguments,

concerns and considerations. This makes them easier to examine and question. Starting by stating your position can be more challenging and make you feel more exposed, but it does make for a clearer conversation:

ANNE: Do you think we should stop Sam going out with Peter?

TARIK: Yes, I think we should.

ANNE: Why do you think that?

TARIK: Because of the trouble they got into last time they went out together. Peter's a nice enough kid, but some of the things he gets up to are a bad influence on Sam. I think it would be a good idea if we don't allow it for a while … three months, say? What do you think?

In the second version of the conversation it's much clearer where Tarik stands, and what arguments he has for his position. There's a clear 'domino fit' between his answers and Anne's questions.

A while ago I was invited to take part in a discussion on *Kramcast*, a podcast on theology, philosophy and politics presented and produced by Mark Eikema.[2] We got on well and the conversation flowed freely before, during and after the recording. For almost two hours we spoke about asking questions, why it's something we often avoid, why we're so bad at it and what the world would be like if we paid it a little more attention. Mark agreed that it would be good if we asked each other more – and, above all, better – questions, with the aim of improving the quality of our conversations.

During the podcast I recounted the lunchtime experience I describe at the beginning of the book – the conversation about having kids in which the childless people at the table were passed over. It was a topic we returned to when the recording was finished, and I shared my doubts and thoughts about whether or not I should start a family of my own. Mark said it's strange how we assume there must be a major reason for someone *not* to have kids, yet we rarely stop to wonder why people *do* have kids.

Mark spoke about his own children: how much he enjoyed life with them, but also how exhausting and challenging it could be. He said he could never have imagined the impact of parenthood beforehand and could certainly appreciate a life without children. At one point I asked him, 'Faced with that choice again, would you do the same?' An intimate question, of course, one that gives rise to a certain amount of tension. Answering it honestly puts you in a vulnerable position, but I felt that the contact between us was open enough to be that direct.

Mark started talking. 'Well, when I look at where we are now and who we were when we were making the choice …' and so on.

My question was a yes-or-no question. If you want to dig deeper in a conversation and focus clearly on the matter at hand – and in this case, we both did – then the first answer should be yes or no, before going in search of nuance. But that's something we're not used to doing, especially when things get personal. And let's face it, questions don't get much more personal than whether or not you regret having kids.

We had just spent two hours exploring the art of conversation and asking good questions. So when Mark looked at me and stopped talking, I said, 'You realise that was a yes-or-no question, don't you?'

'Oh … right! And here I am rabbiting on. Normally I'd get away with an answer like that, but not now, of course. Okay then, let me focus and do my best to answer your question.'

I kept quiet.

'Yes, if I had to do it all again, I'd make the same choice. Because if I look at what my life is like right now …'

What followed was a clear and nuanced story that gave a good basis for asking questions and offered room for new insights. Mark had never answered this question for himself in this way and, in doing so – and giving himself time to think and focus on his response – he hit upon views and thoughts he didn't even know he had.

It takes two

For a good conversation, you want the dominoes to match up. And you want the players to take turns. You don't want someone spilling all their dominoes on the table at once and crowding out the other player. All being well, you don't just speak to hear the sound of your own voice, you speak to be heard by someone else. Rather than getting caught up in your own story, you need to maintain contact with the person you are talking to. You do this non-verbally, of course, through eye contact and body language, but also with what you have to say. People often weigh in with a monologue peppered with fancy words selected, either consciously or unconsciously, in an effort to impress the other person, to show their credentials or to appear smart. But that's not a conversation, it's an all-singing, all-dancing one-person show. Launching into a monologue is often only fascinating and fun for one person: the speaker.

One of Socrates's rules of conversation is to speak briefly and concisely. In the dialogue with Protagoras as described in Hans Bolten's article 'The Socratic dialogue as a tool for team reflection', Socrates asks his conversation partner to stop indulging in incomprehensible monologues, claiming he simply cannot follow them.

SOCRATES: Protagoras, I have a wretched memory, and when anyone makes a long speech to me I never remember what they are talking about. As then, if I had been deaf, and you were going to converse with me, you would have had to raise your voice; so now, having such

a bad memory, I will ask you to cut your answers shorter,
if you would take me with you.

PROTAGORAS: What do you mean? How am I to
shorten my answers? Shall I make them too short?

SOCRATES: Certainly not.

PROTAGORAS: But short enough?

SOCRATES: Yes.[3]

'It's a restriction that irritates Protagoras,' Bolten writes.
'He is used to speaking as he sees fit: with an abundance of
words designed to impress. That, after all, is what sets him
apart from other debaters.' He continues to explain how
Protagoras has no intention of complying with Socrates's
wishes. Eventually, Socrates plays the trump card and threatens to walk out:

SOCRATES: Protagoras, I do not wish to force the
conversation upon you if you had rather not, but when
you are willing to argue with me in such a way that I can
follow you, then I will argue with you. [...] But I see that
you are disinclined, and as I have an engagement which
will prevent my staying to hear you at greater length (for
I have to be in another place), I will depart; although I
should have liked to have heard you.[4]

Bolten then describes how the crowd that gathered to
listen to the two men are aghast, and they try to persuade

the pair to continue the conversation. Eventually Protagoras agrees and commits to saying the things he wants to say in a brief, concise and understandable manner, as Socrates requested. Bolten writes:

> Only then can Socrates examine the issue that forms the meat of the conversation between the two men: are learning, wisdom, bravery, justice and piety different words for one and the same thing, virtue, or are they five essentially different things?[5]

FOLLOWING THROUGH WITH YOUR QUESTIONS

One of the most frequently asked questions in the courses and workshops I give about asking questions is 'How can I follow through with my questions?' Asking good follow-up questions gives your conversations greater depth. It takes you beyond the superficiality of everyday small talk. You get to know the other person better and give them room to show their vulnerable side. But how do you set about following through? Where do you start? What aspects of the conversation lend themselves to follow-up questions? What methods exist for asking these questions? How do you keep on asking without stepping on toes? How can you confront someone by asking follow-up questions?

What following through is and isn't

Following through with your questions is about making sure that you explore a statement, point of view or story more deeply. It's not about taking a wider view or adding new narratives or new concepts. Instead it's about delving deeper into what's already on the table. You can follow through by asking about the reasons behind a point of view. You can ask for examples or explore other strands of that particular topic. If you drift off-topic and ask a question that's not about the one you're discussing but touches on a relatively unrelated area, then you're not following through, but starting a new conversation.

Following through can have the same effect as asking why – it can pressure people into thinking they have to defend themselves. In a way, of course, that's exactly what you *are* doing. You're asking someone to substantiate their point of view or statement. They aren't going to get away with a throwaway remark like 'People on benefits just don't want to work' as long as you are there to ask them to back up their statement with arguments and evidence.

That's exactly why so many of us don't follow through with our questions: we don't want to make life difficult for the other person, preferring to keep the mood light and relations amicable. 'Who am I to call someone else to account? Is it my job to investigate other people's arguments and reasons?'

Well, why not? Since when is it a bad idea to ask someone what they really think or what they meant to say? Since when are we supposed to nod and smile and not take a genuine interest in the evidence that underpins someone's views and arguments? In following through with a question, you're asking the other person to take responsibility for their statements. Statements that hopefully (though not always) have a foundation worth exploring. I believe we err on the side of caution when it comes to following through. By not asking enough questions, we let our conversations slide into a string of platitudes or ill-considered assertions with precious little in the way of evidence to back them up.

Of course your success in asking good follow-up questions relies on maintaining your Socratic attitude. If your questions are accompanied by a judgemental gaze or tone of voice, you will achieve the opposite of what you set out to do. You have to be genuinely curious about the thinking behind what the other person has to say, and suspend your own opinions on the matter. Sometimes the simple fact of responding to an answer with another question can be enough to encourage your conversation partner to reflect: 'Does what I'm saying really ring true? I assumed I knew what I was talking about, but maybe I haven't thought this through enough ...'

Following through = analytical thinking and listening

To follow through with genuine and effective questions, you first have to listen attentively to exactly what someone is saying. That means not being too personally invested in the content, not being concerned with your own point of view, not setting out to convince or enter into a debate. Listen purely and Socratically to the surface features of the language being used. Shelve your empathy for a while and steer clear of comforting, advising or fixing. Above all, be curious about what's behind a statement or assertion. Your focus lies with two fundamental questions: 'What is this person literally saying?' and 'What is the thinking behind these words?'

Successfully following through with your questions requires you to create a little distance – distance from your conversation partner and distance from the topic of conversation. Ask yourself what kind of statement the other person is making, and consider whether this new statement is consistent with what they said a moment ago or whether they have just contradicted themselves. Registering these aspects of a conversation, instead of getting carried away by its content, makes it much easier for you to ask better questions.

Ask the obvious

The easiest way to follow through is by questioning what appears to be self-explanatory. Often we fill things in for ourselves during the course of a conversation, convinced that we understand what the other person means. But if you listen Socratically and focus on the language being used, questions will quickly start to pop into your head.

If someone says, 'Teachers should stop whining and be glad they've got a decent job', it's our gut instinct either to nod along – 'Yes, I couldn't agree more' – or take a stand – 'Well, my aunt is a teacher and she's says it's actually a very tough profession.' We seldom think to ask a question. But if you listen Socratically and question what seems self-evident, you might ask, 'What is it these teachers are saying?' or 'What makes you say they have a decent job?'

The other person may automatically go on the defensive and start sputtering things like, 'Well, you only have to look at the news …', but if you persist in your questioning, inevitably the other person will have to look at their own implicit, unconscious beliefs and make them explicit.

Exercise: questioning what seems self-evident

Ask someone to do this exercise with you. Get them to write down a viewpoint that they take for granted. Maybe they have a strong opinion about congestion charges, #MeToo, politics or religion. Get them to select one of these and formulate their position as an assertion or argument.

For example:

Parents should have their children vaccinated for the health of society as a whole. Parents who oppose vaccination should think less about themselves and more about the common good.

Then make a conscious effort to apply your own handbrake: don't think about whether you agree or disagree, or start coming up with ways to offer your own option on the matter or to change their mind. Your only aim is to investigate the self-evident elements of the argument. Embrace those supposedly stupid questions, because these questions cast doubt on the seemingly obvious parts of a statement. For example:

- Are parents who don't want to vaccinate their kids only thinking of themselves?
- Why is it important to think about the common good?
- How does vaccinating children benefit the health of society?
- Is it wrong to think of yourself?
- How much should you think about yourself and how much about others?

Two ways to follow through

Generally speaking, you can take two approaches with your follow-up questions: you can focus on the other person's thinking in order to explore the presuppositions, assumptions and ideas behind it, or you can work with them to examine a position that is diametrically opposed to their own.

Questioning their thinking	Examining the other point of view
How can you be sure?	Is that what everyone thinks?
What argument do you have?	What would someone who disagrees with you say?
What are you basing that on?	Could it be any other way?

Questions aimed at the other person's position involve digging deeper into their thinking. What are they basing their statement on? What presuppositions underlie that view? How have they structured their thinking and is it a construction that makes sense?

Asking questions about the opposing point of view calls for a certain degree of flexibility from the person you are having the conversation with. Can they use their cognitive empathy to step into someone else's shoes and understand the opposite opinion?

There's no golden rule for when to choose which approach. But it is useful to have a clear understanding of the position expressed by the other person before you invite them to explore alternative options.

Exercise: two-way follow through

The next time you hear someone make a statement that you want to question and follow through on, begin by being aware of these two approaches. First, seek to interrogate the other person's own way of thinking: 'How do you know that?' 'What makes you say that?' 'How does that work exactly?'

Once you are sincerely satisfied that you understand their thinking (which is not the same as agreeing or disagreeing with it!), change direction and explore the opposite position: 'Is that always the case?' 'In what circumstances might things work differently?' 'How would someone who has experienced X, Y or Z think about this?'

Echo: the simplest way to follow through

The echo question is one of those staples that you can use any time, anywhere. Especially if you're not sure what to ask next, but still want to follow through with your questions about what someone has said. The echo question keeps you listening from the second position or 'You' intention (which we covered in Part Two), without making suggestions or introducing new concepts. It stops you filling in or making assumptions. The echo question is an ideal way to stay focused on the other person while digging that little bit deeper and exploring what they have to say. Your question should ring as clear and simple as an echo from a well: use exactly the same words as they did. Not a rough approximation or a paraphrase, but a literal repetition.

When a colleague says, 'I had a talk with Jim the other day and it was quite an ordeal', you can ask 'What was quite an ordeal about it?' If a friend complains about her boyfriend and says, 'Chris is such a loser', you might ask 'What makes Chris such a loser?' You literally bounce the other person's words back at them, just as your own words might echo back at you from the bottom of a well.

A few examples of good and bad echo questions:

That meeting went on for ever.

DON'T ASK: Why was the meeting so long?

What was the problem?

DO ASK: Why did the meeting go on for ever?

Hank's mother was up to her usual tricks.

DON'T ASK: What did she do?

What did she say this time?

DO ASK: What do you mean 'She was up to her usual tricks'?

I think that's such a ridiculous thing to do.

DON'T ASK: How come?

What was so idiotic about what they did?

DO ASK: What was such a ridiculous thing to do? Why do you think it was such a ridiculous thing to do?

In each example the good-echo question sticks very closely to what the other person said. There's no paraphrasing, there are no new concepts. Repeating their own words back at them means the other person feels heard and is able to continue with their own train of thought.

It can feel a little strange at first. A participant on one of my courses remarked, 'But this feels so fake. So what if I phrase it differently? I mean, the other person still gets it, right?' However, his partner in this exercise didn't feel that way at all. Hearing an 'echo question' made him feel that he had been understood and was being given every opportunity to tell his story his way.

Of course, you can't use this ploy in response to every statement for the next ten minutes. Not without turning into the parrot everyone would happily strangle. But try not to worry about that too much, and feel free to experiment with echo questions. You're far more likely to feel like a parrot yourself, before your conversation partner starts to see you that way.

Following through on concepts

A statement or a question often centres on a single concept: the crux, the thing that really matters. A concept is a theme, an idea, the issue at hand. It usually takes the form of no more than one word that hovers above a statement or question like an invisible shop sign. Learning to recognise concepts helps you ask better follow-up questions and distinguish main issues from minor details.

For instance, to go back to an earlier example, someone might say, 'You have to let parents decide for themselves whether to have their children vaccinated. That's not something you can impose from on high.' The central concept hovering over this statement is autonomy. This appears to be what the speaker sees as the most important issue when it comes to vaccination. For them, that's what at stake.

Someone else might emphasise another aspect: 'Vaccination is something that needs to be regulated and managed centrally. Suppose no one had their kids vaccinated: we'd soon be overrun by all kinds of diseases that are currently more or less under control.' Here, the central concept for this person is control.

We have two very different positions on the same issue. Looking at the underlying concepts reveals in no uncertain terms how easily clashes could arise: autonomy and control are each other's opposites. Learning how concepts work, learning to identify a central concept, gives you real clarity. In your own thinking, but also in conversations, and certainly when you want to ask good follow-up questions.

In response to the above statements, you might ask:

- Is parental autonomy paramount?
- Is it bad to give up a measure of autonomy?
- What would be the consequences if we gave parents full autonomy on vaccination?

Or:

- Where does control stop and autonomy begin?
- How far should you go in controlling what parents do and don't do?

Imagine a friend told you, 'I've agreed with my sister Janet that, from now on, we'll take it in turns to call our mother. Mum's alone a lot of the time and Janet still lives quite close, while I live further away. To be honest, I think Janet could do more for Mum. It's so much easier for her.'

Consider what concept your friend is actually expressing here. What are they really getting at? If you can grasp that central concept, you can gain a much clearer picture of what to ask. If you simply started asking questions at random, the chances are you'd pick up on an aspect that reflects your own interests. That increases your chance of losing touch with the other person's train of thought, while the whole point is to stay as close to it as possible.

Exercise: identifying concepts

Take a look at the following statements, try to identify the central concept and express it as one word.

1. Statues of public figures like Cecil Rhodes should be left alone. They're part of our nation's history. That's not something we can just turn our backs on.

2. Becoming a vegetarian was a conscious choice for me. I think it's wrong to slaughter innocent animals for our own pleasure.

3. There should be vending machines where women can get tampons and sanitary towels free of charge. It's unfair that women should have to spend more money than men simply because they are women.

4. Free speech was, and is, an important precondition for citizens to participate fully in the public debate. Without free speech, all kinds of abuses would never be exposed. Without free speech, citizens would have no opportunity to influence government.

Exercise: follow-up questions about concepts

Find yourself a newspaper or magazine that features an interview, an opinion piece or a letters page. Read a statement or a paragraph and try to pick out the central concept. Then think of three questions you could ask the person who made the statement. This exercise will help you get quicker at recognising concepts in a conversation so that you can go on to ask good questions that get to the point.

CONFRONTING WITH YOUR QUESTIONS

The ability to confront someone with a well-chosen question in conversation, one of those questions that hits home and instantly makes a person think about what they have just said: it's a great skill to master, mainly because it makes many a conversation partner think. But how do you go about it? How do you ask a question that compels someone to reflect on what they are saying? And maybe even makes them aware of their own bullshit, inconsistent thinking or ill-considered statements?

Practical philosopher Ariane van Heijningen presents us with these tips and ideas about confronting with questions:

> We often see confronting other people about their own statements as a risk, and worry it might lead to a quarrel or conflict. In our perception, it's a short step from confrontation to discord, strife and bother. When it comes to confrontation, we cling to quite a few assumptions:
>
> - Confrontation leads to conflict – the other person will probably feel hurt by my question, have no desire to answer it and is bound to respond defensively.
> - Confrontation creates tension – it jeopardises the relationship.
> - I only have the right to confront someone if I'm very knowledgeable about the subject at hand and believe I know more about it than they do.

But once you have made the Socratic attitude your own and ask your questions non-judgementally, confronting someone with a question needn't be that difficult at all.

What is confrontation?

In its most literal sense, to confront means to take up position across from another person. And in essence, that's exactly what confrontation is, no more and no less. You return what you receive. You mirror what you hear.

The Socratic approach to confrontation amounts to nothing more than handing someone's own statements back to them so that they can ponder them for themselves. It's not about occupying the higher ground and taking someone down a peg or two. Or insisting that you're right and they're wrong and dishing out a firm rap on the knuckles. It's about listening attentively and giving back.

So when is confrontation the right option? You may want to confront someone with their own statements if:

- They are being unclear.
- They use a lot of words but don't actually say much.
- They contradict themselves.
- They make an error of reasoning.

This take on confrontation also suggests that you don't need to be much of an expert on what the other person is saying. You tune in and listen using the techniques you've learned in this book: the 'what-exactly-do-you-mean' third approach to listening. An approach that is sensitive to surface features, operates at language level and responds to someone's tone of voice, the structure of their argument, the concepts they are appealing to and any contradictions that might emerge. The less you know, the better placed you are to question the obvious, and often that's exactly what gets the other person thinking.

But steer clear of this kind of confrontation if:

- You just want to win a debate.
- The other person is getting on your nerves and you want to let them know it.
- You're not in the mood, might never see the other person again and don't really care whether they talk a lot of nonsense or not.

If you go ahead and confront someone when you are irritated, or simply want to prove that you're right and they're wrong, then your confrontation will probably end up sounding like a reproach. And that generates exactly what you don't want – a quarrel or conflict. Confrontation by questioning thrives when it's accompanied by calm, empathic neutrality and a healthy dose of attentive listening.

How to use a question to confront

So how exactly do you confront someone while keeping your Socratic cool? In a one-to-one conversation? One way of using a question to confront is simply to repeat the other person's statement, or part of it. This operates on the same principle as the echo questions we covered earlier.

For example:
- Everyone in debt is bad with money.
- Everyone?

Or:
- Ben is so incredibly arrogant!
- Arrogant?

Another simple way to confront someone is to adopt the attitude of a naive, astonished listener and to literally ask for an explanation.

For example:
- People in debt are bad with money.
- They're bad with money? What exactly do you mean by that?

Or:
- With all those women banging on about #MeToo, it won't be long before a man can't do anything any more!
- I don't get it. How does women talking about #MeToo mean a man can't do anything any more?

Or:

- You know what these people are like!
- No, I don't, actually. What are they like?

In instances where the other person hasn't answered your question, you can confront them by telling them exactly that and then repeating your question so that they can have a go. This involves listening closely and, of course, spotting whether or not someone answers your question, as well as any shortcomings in whatever answer they do give you.

YOU: What is taking responsibility?
THEM: It has to do with courage.
YOU: That doesn't answer the question. You've mentioned something it has to do with. But what *is* taking responsibility?

Or:

YOU: What's so cool about this job?
THEM: Well, it's a job I've wanted for so long!
YOU: That doesn't answer the question. It tells me how you felt about the job before you got it, but it doesn't say anything about the job itself. What's so cool about this job?

When someone sends a torrent of words your way to blunt the point of your question, hang on in there. Don't let them get away with bamboozling you, and keep asking for a clear and unambiguous answer. This is another form of confrontation.

> For example:
> YOU: How are you getting on at work?
> THEM: Well, you know that feeling when you think you want something, but then again you don't really want it at all, like your heart's saying one thing and your head's saying something else, because you know you've made these agreements with people when actually all you want to do is get out from under them, but you don't know how and it doesn't feel right?
> YOU: What are you trying to say?

Ariane van Heijningen writes this on her blog, about confronting with questions:

> Confrontation is simply about giving back what you receive. That's all it is. You're just pointing something out. Marking the limits of what someone is saying and helping them sharpen their own thinking. We're not used to confronting without judgement, with no ulterior motive, and with no other purpose than simply working together to become a little wiser. Yet it's precisely our lack of judgement and ulterior motive – as unfamiliar as it may feel – that makes a confrontation nothing more

and nothing less than giving back what someone else has brought to the table. Pure, simple and clear as that.[6]

Confrontational questions can generate a bit of tension, and there's nothing wrong with that. After all you are inviting, perhaps even compelling, the other person to think about what they are really saying, and asking them to clarify, substantiate and take responsibility for their words. But no one has ever been worse off for having done that.

Even so, our unease persists: 'Isn't it an inconsiderate thing to do? Confronting someone like that?' This is a question I'm often asked. Nevertheless, at the end of the day I think it would be far more inconsiderate to the other person and the conversation you're having – not to mention to yourself and the wider world – if you let them go on uncritically believing in their own bullshit. Becoming wiser together is largely about separating sense from nonsense.

Exercise: confronting with your question

Over the next few days take a critical look at the news and note when someone is unclear, contradicts themselves, launches into a long story without getting to the point or trips over their own thinking. In each case, think about what kind of question you might ask to confront the other person with their ramblings, vagueness, contradictions or wrong-headedness and to encourage them to reflect on it.

Once you're feeling confident, try it out in a one-to-one conversation. And if that works and you feel happy shifting up a gear, try asking someone a question to confront them during a meeting or group discussion. But remember to pay extra attention to your own attitude: remain open, without judgement, and keep observing and listening with wonder.

FOLLOWING THROUGH: A 'WHAT-IF' QUESTION AS A SHOT IN THE ARM

If you want to show someone the other side of an issue, expand their thinking a little and give them some extra headspace, a sincere 'what-if' question can sometimes work wonders. It can come as a bit of a surprise and, consequently, can set someone's thinking in motion, very often inviting an answer that even the person giving the answer didn't see coming.

Knowing what you think lets you decide if you want to think it

Brenda signed up for one of my first 'Philosophy in Everyday Life' courses. There were twelve people in the group and we met every week to develop our practical philosophical skills. We had discussions, did thought exercises and trained our Socratic questioning techniques.

One evening we were working on judgement. We often judge situations directly and intuitively, without exactly knowing what our judgement is based on, but an outspoken opinion is actually an end point and the arguments in support of that judgement remain unclear. When other people question your initial, intuitive judgement and you become aware of the mental construct you have built for yourself, you can either consciously choose to stick with your judgement or to abandon it. That evening Brenda did the latter.

I showed the group a somewhat 'edgy' wedding photo. The bride and groom had decided to strike a pose that was playful, to say the least. The picture was taken from the bushes and shows the groom standing with his back to the camera and the trousers of his dark-blue suit around his knees. Only part of the bride's white veil and dress are visible, but it's clear that she's kneeling in front of him, and there's a definite suggestion to the scene of al-fresco fellatio.

The questions I put to the group were: 'Does the photograph go too far? If yes, then why? And if no, why not?' Everyone was invited to give their opinion and provide their arguments. Brenda's first verdict was a resounding 'Yes'. She felt that the picture went way too far and found it completely unacceptable, yet she couldn't put her finger on precisely why. Her response seemed to have something to do with romance and a sense that it shouldn't be portrayed that way.

At one point I asked her, 'What if the bride and groom hadn't been photographed in their wedding outfits, but in their everyday casual clothes. Would the photo go too far then?'

Brenda didn't even hesitate. 'No!' she exclaimed. 'Of course not!' As soon as she heard herself say the words, she clasped her hand to her mouth, startled by the sudden realisation of a hidden value, one she had never even been aware she held: deep down she clearly felt that a bride and groom should be depicted as chaste.

Brenda was shocked to discover her rather traditional hidden belief. She was in a same-sex relationship – married with two children – and saw herself as a very progressive and open-minded person. She was taken aback at this instinctive value judgement, as she felt it didn't reflect who she believed she was as a person. Later she explained that she'd had a very conservative upbringing and suspected that the link between bridal couples and chastity was more to do with her parents' mindset than her own. This example gave her a clear insight into her own thinking and what it was based on, and from there she was able to decide that this was not the kind of view she wanted to hold or, indeed, the kind of person she wanted to be.

When I asked her to look at the picture again, she laughed. She still didn't think it was a particularly good photo or in the best of taste, but this time she was in a different frame of mind and was able to make an informed judgement – one she felt much more at home with.

By opening yourself up to focused questioning, you sometimes encounter opinions, judgements, assumptions or values that you never even knew you had. The Socratic process can sometimes be a confrontational and even painful process, but afterwards, when the result of your thinking is out in the open, you're better able to reassess your response and see whether it does justice to who you are and who you want to be. It gives you room to explore an issue and the chance to decide afresh; to reshape your identity and make clear, thoughtful choices. It's an approach that allows you to shake off old thinking patterns – fixed values and outmoded opinions, inherited views – and remould them in your own image. For that process to work, you need good, in-depth questions.

Exercise: ask a 'what-if' question

If you're talking to someone and suspect they might be getting a little bogged down and could use some extra headspace, try asking a 'what-if' question. To do this, it helps if you stick to their wording as much as possible when formulating your question:

> THEM: I was so nervous at that party last night after Ramona showed up.
> YOU: What if Ramona hadn't come to the party? Would you still have been as nervous?

OPEN YOURSELF UP TO QUESTIONING

The art of asking questions is not something you acquire overnight. It takes time, practice and training. The attitude of wonder you have towards others is something you will also have to develop when looking at yourself. When do you come out with assertions that make very little sense? When do you throw up a verbal smokescreen to conceal what's really going on? When do you contradict yourself? Are you capable of dissecting, analysing and critically questioning your own thinking? And do you allow others to criticise you? Are you brave enough to go back on your previous viewpoint, explore new perspectives and perhaps even change your mind entirely?

You develop a genuine, open attitude of wonder by being open to questions yourself. By daring to doubt your own opinions, beliefs and assumptions. When you dare to question and have doubts about yourself, you automatically become milder and more open towards others.

Opening *yourself* up to questioning is perhaps the most important condition for mastering the art of asking questions. How can you question others if you're not prepared to think openly and curiously about yourself? When you have experienced *elenchus* or *aporia* a number of times, you'll be able to understand other people's responses to Socratic questioning.

Above all, if you are to awaken new insights in someone else, you have to do your best to embody the Socratic attitude and live by its example. That means questioning yourself and what you say time and time again, and inviting others to question you. Be ruthless in your critical self-examination, avoid the temptation to let yourself off the hook. And when someone else questions you, take their questions to heart. There's no value in avoiding them or smothering them with wordplay. Throwing up a smokescreen of words, and dancing around the question, only disguises your own insecurity or inconsistencies and doesn't make you any wiser. Be brave enough to doubt what you think you know for sure, and embrace not-knowing. Have an opinion and take a stand and then substantiate it, but remain open to changing your mind when it becomes clear that you should. Kindle your own agile perspective, and then help to light that same flame in others.

But what about me? When do I get to have my say?

Throughout this book you have been concerned with the other person. You've learned how to listen effectively and how to develop an enquiring Socratic attitude. You've tossed your own agenda out of the window and dived headlong into the other person's thinking. You know how to ask questions, how to follow through with your questioning, how to recognise critical points, drill down into the detail, move up to abstraction and pick out key concepts.

Maybe all this has you wondering whether you're still allowed to speak your own mind. When exactly do you get to have your say? Doesn't your point of view deserve a little air time? How do you make the transition from the other person's views to sharing your own ideas?

First understand, then be understood

We all want a bit of understanding. But if we spend all our time broadcasting our own views, the end result is that no one feels understood at all. Most of us are perfectly capable of launching our own opinions at others, yet few of us fully grasp how to be receptive, slow things down and examine what's really being said. That's why this book is devoted almost entirely to developing those receptive and analytical skills. I'm convinced that if we get better at them, our conversations will improve enormously – as will the level and quality of public debate – if people become better at handling painful discussions and clashes of opinion, however polarised.

Once you really understand another person and can connect with their way of thinking, you can make room for your narrative and your point of view. After all, you don't just want to vent an opinion. You want the other person to actually hear what you have to say and take it in, right? Well, in order to do that, first you need to build a bridge.

A few principles of bridge-building

A bridge is only as strong as the foundations laid on either side. That's why you start by investing so much time, attention and energy in listening and unravelling what the other person is thinking. When the basis for understanding is firm on the far bank, you can then begin construction and invite the other person across to hear and explore your side of the story. The bridge – that invitation – can easily take the form of another question.

Imagine sitting at a table with a friend or colleague, having questioned and explored their viewpoint. There's every chance that at some point they will ask, 'What do you think?

What's your take on all this?' Even if they don't, you can make a little space for your own thoughts in the form of a proposal: 'I've got a few ideas about this, too. Would you like to hear them?' or 'Interesting. I can't say I agree with you on everything, though. Shall I tell you how I see it?'

This is not simply about asking permission to have your say. You're doing something far more important – you're opening up the other person's mind to being receptive. They have just spent a while expressing their own thoughts and ideas, and moving from broadcasting your point of view to absorbing someone else's means switching roles. That sudden switch is quicker and easier to navigate once you know that another point of view is heading your way.

That's a step we often skip. We listen patiently to the other person in the conversation, sometimes ask them a question or two and then treat them to a barrelful of our own opinions, with very little preamble in which to prepare to switch roles and make a smooth transition from speaker to listener. By easing from one phase of conversation to the next, you'll start to experience greater clarity and flow: it becomes clear whose opinion is under examination, and even clearer which points you agree and disagree on.

Exercise: bridge-building

Have a conversation in which you start by examining the other person's views. Follow through with your questions and listen carefully to the answers. Maybe at some point the other person will ask you what you think. Until that moment comes, see if you can continue asking questions and stick with what the other person is saying, and practise only offering your own opinion when the other person invites you to. If they don't ask you to share your views, create your own bridge with a phrase like:

- I have one or two ideas about this, too. Can I put them to you?
- Do you want to know what I think about this?
- What you've been saying has given me a few insights of my own. Shall I share them with you?

Once you've made your bridge, keep looking and listening attentively. What effect does it have on the other person, and on the conversation that follows?

Yeah, but it doesn't always work that way …

Once, at a party, someone asked me about the book I was writing. I explained it was about asking questions, having deeper conversations and exploring your own thinking and the other person's.

'That's all well and good,' one man said, 'but it doesn't always work that way, does it? I have this one friend who never has much to say. I ask him questions, but he never seems that interested. So I don't really feel the need to follow through and dig deeper. I mean, why bother if he's not as invested in the conversation as I am?'

He had a point, of course. Why would you pour your energy into a conversation if the other person turns out to have no real interest in your ideas and opinions?

To be honest, that's a hard one for me to answer. For me personally, what someone else thinks is interesting by definition. I enjoy trying to get to the bottom of things and practising my own questioning skills. Even with people who talk nonsense, whose views seem simplistic and who could easily get on my nerves. I'm interested in questioning them and discovering their logic, which often bears little resemblance to my own. Asking them questions broadens my view of the rest of the world. By understanding one person, I can also begin to better understand other people who appear to hold similar views. I sometimes view that one person and their views as representative of a larger group whose ways of thinking I'm getting to grips with; a new kind of perspective that was unknown or even alien to me before. It's such a fascinating and worthwhile process that the need to make myself heard tends to fall away.

That's why I don't always mind if there's not much energy or interest from the other person in what I have to say. My enjoyment comes from immersing myself in how the other person thinks, and so it's not always important for me to make it clear where I stand, or whether I convince people of

my own views or opinions. I've had very rewarding conversations with people who think completely differently from
me, without once sharing my own views, mainly by engaging
with their way of thinking from a place of genuine interest
and wonder. The process of comparing and contrasting those
views with my own tends to come much later – on my drive
home, or while I'm eating dinner.

But of course I'd be lying if I said I wasn't familiar with
what the man in the party had experienced. You're eager to
have a good conversation with someone, but it's abundantly
clear that they have little interest, and so you end up doing all
the heavy lifting. At such a point it is worth asking yourself:
'How much of a problem is their lack of interest, and how
much energy am I willing to invest in this conversation? Do
I need the other person to be as interested in me as I am in
them? Do I feel my interest in them ought to be reciprocated,
or am I able to enjoy simply asking questions?'

In situations like this, my mother always says, 'Choose
your battles.' You don't *have* to talk to everyone. That pomp-
ous cousin who's always telling the same stories at family
get-togethers? Give him a wide berth if you're not in the
mood. The colleague you have nothing in common with,
and who seems to sap your energy as soon as they walk
into the room? Of course you're under no obligation to
have a Socratic conversation with them, either. Keeping an
eye on whether you feel your energy rise or dissipate when
you talk to someone seems like a very healthy instinct to

me. But that said, who knows what hidden gems you might come across if you let go of all your preconceptions about the other person and give it a go, even if it's only for five minutes. Don't be afraid to go on a Socratic expedition into the mind of someone who's not that interested in you, or whose thinking seems so far removed from your own, or someone you may not even like at all. Enter into a conversation without burdening yourself with high expectations and you may well be pleasantly surprised. What's the worst that can happen? You might pick up a new insight or simply receive confirmation of what you thought already.

I see a sincere interest in another person as a gift. For them. And maybe for yourself, too. I firmly believe that today's world needs better conversations in which we seek to become wiser together, instead of convincing the other person that we are right and they are wrong; conversations that make time for new perspectives and insights, and in which we want to understand someone else before being understood ourselves. I believe that a good conversation starts with a good question. And a good question starts with an attitude of curiosity and wonder, and a genuine desire to know. The attitude embodied by our old friend Socrates.

My own mini-Socrates is right here beside me on the couch. His sneakers are mucky after a jog around the park, his cape is mud-spattered. I look at him and ask: 'Socrates, do you think this book will do any good? Will it inspire people and help them have better conversations? Do you think it might help make the world a little better?'

'Don't ask me.' Socrates looks back at me and shrugs. 'Time will tell … There's still a long way to go. But this is a good start.'

Afterword

A BOOK IS LIKE a stage play. It's never really finished. I should know – I've written a few! The text may be fixed and printed on the page but the thinking never stops, the ideas keep developing.

The colours and mood of a play change, the more it's performed. By the end of a run, the details, nuances and characterisation are never quite what they were at the start. The interaction with the audience enriches a performance and enables it to evolve.

I believe books work in much the same way. In contact with you – the reader – new ideas, insights and questions take shape; new ways of thinking about the topics covered in these pages. You can follow this process at www.socratesopsneakers.nl and www.denksmederij.nl. There you'll find articles, videos, exercises and a calendar of events. And of course you are welcome to ask questions or share your thoughts and ideas.

I look forward to entering into a dialogue with you there.

Acknowledgements

A N IDEA CAN only benefit from being questioned and challenged. The same is true of a book. A whole host of people deserve my thanks for their invaluable contributions, ideas, critical questions, encouragement and heartfelt support.

First of all, to everyone who was willing to share their story with me, to answer my questions and join me on my search. Many of your stories can be found in this book. Thank you for your openness and generosity.

To Matthijs, my love and my sparring partner, for reading every word and being there every step of the way. Thank you for being the whetstone that always makes me sharper and gets me thinking more clearly.

To my mother, a never-ending source of wisdom in connection, questioning and contact.

To my sister Anne: what a treasure to have someone by my side who knows me through and through.

To my father, Wim Wiss, who steadfastly reads my every contribution, article and blog, listens to every podcast and shares everything on his Facebook page – with the occasional critical note and spelling correction.

To my teachers Hans Bolten, Kristof van Rossem, Oscar Brenifier, and Karin de Galan: your ideas, lessons and theories are woven into the fabric of this book. Thank you for everything I have been privileged to learn from you and still hope to learn.

To Floor Overmars of literary agency Sebes & Bisseling: thank you for your very first email, your enthusiasm and your rock-steady confidence in the value of this book.

To my Dutch publishing team at Ambo|Anthos: your guidance made this book so much better than if I had written it on my own. Thank you.

I would also like to send out a big thanks to my English publisher Penguin Random House UK and my editor there, and to my German publisher Kösel-Verlag and my Korean publisher Korean DongYang Books Corporation, for their trust in publishing this book in their countries. With your help in translating this book, deeper and more meaningful conversations are available to an even bigger audience.

To my co-readers from the word go: Iris Posthouwer, Annemiek Laarhoven, Ariane van Heijningen, Sigrid van Iersel, Lars van Kessel, Stella Amesz, Rose Spearman, Nynke Brugman and Ruben Klerkx. Thank you for your tips, advice, critical notes and your words of praise and encouragement. Without your feedback, this book would never have become what it is.

To everyone who offered their support though email, LinkedIn, Facebook and Instagram – thank you. You may not have realised it, but in moments of self-doubt, your support was truly heart-warming. At times it felt like having my own personal cheerleading squad.

And last but not least, huge thanks to you, dear reader. Thank you for taking the time to read this book. For your willingness to immerse yourself in the art of asking good questions and your readiness to think more clearly, express your thoughts, have better conversations and search for greater depth and connection. I can't change the nature of our conversations on my own, just by writing a book. But together, one good conversation at a time, we can make things happen. You are an essential part of that process. Thank you for being here.

Notes

1 Rainer Maria Rilke, *Letters to a Young Poet*, trans. M. D. Herter Norton (New York: W. W. Norton & Company, 1993), Fourth Letter, pp. 33–5, www.thedailyphilosopher.org/daily/000007.php

INTRODUCTION

1 Rumi, *The Big Red Book: The Great Masterpiece Celebrating Mystical Love and Friendship*, trans. Coleman Barks (San Francisco: HarperOne, 2011), p. 367
2 Lammert Kamphuis, *Filosofie voor een weergaloos leven* (Amsterdam: De Bezige Bij, 2018)
3 Plato, *The Dialogues of Plato*, trans. Benjamin Jowett, Vol. 1, 2nd edn (Oxford: Clarendon Press, 1875), p. 289
4 'Socrates dood: de oerknal voor de filosofie', *Filosofie*, 10 June 2016, www.filosofie.nl/socrates-dood-de-oerknal-voor-de-filosofie/
5 Carolina Lo Galbo, 'Hoe Femke Halsema verbindend werd', *Vrij Nederland*, 23 April 2019, www.vn.nl/femke-halsema-verbindend-burgemeester/

PART ONE: WHY ARE WE SO BAD AT ASKING GOOD QUESTIONS?

1 Plato, *The Dialogues of Plato*, Vol. 1 (1875), p. 362
2 Oscar Wilde, *The Picture of Dorian Gray* (London: Ward Lock, 1891), Preface
3 Huub Buijssen, *Mag ik je geen advies geven? In 6 stappen van probleem naar oplossing met de methode coachende gespreksvoering* (Tilburg: TRED Buijssen Training en Educatie, 2018)
4 Ellen de Visser, 'Waarom je bij problemen beter geen advies kunt geven', *de Volkskrant*, 13 July 2018, www.volkskrant.nl/degids/waarom-je-bij-problemen-beter-geen-advies-kunt-geven~b80bcac7/

5   Adrian F. Ward, 'The Neuroscience of Everybody's Favorite Topic: Why do people spend so much time talking about themselves?', *Scientific American*, 16 July 2013

6   Diana I. Tamir and Jason P. Mitchell, 'Disclosing Information About the Self is Intrinsically Rewarding', *Proceedings of the National Academy of Sciences* (2012), 109.21, pp. 8038–43, www.ncbi.nlm.nih.gov/pmc/journals/2/

7   Anne Neijnens, 'Jan Geurtz: De Spirituele Liefdesrelatie', *De Anne Neijnens Show*, 22 August 2018, soundcloud.com/anneneijnens/jangeurtz

8   Sigrid van Iersel in correspondence with Elke Wiss.

9   Brené Brown, *Braving the Wilderness: The Quest for True Belonging and the Courage to Stand Alone* (New York: Random House, 2017), p. 91

10   www.youtube.com/watch?v=ELD2AwFN9Nc&vl=en

11   *Dit was het nieuws*, broadcast 17 December 2017

12   Nathalie Huigsloot, 'Janine Abbring: "Als je wilt weten waarom God niet bestaat, moet je naar het leven van mijn moeder kijken"', *de Volkskrant Magazine*, 6 July 2018, www.volkskrant.nl/mensen/janine-abbring-als-je-wilt-weten-waarom-god-nietbestaat-moet-je-naar-het-leven-van-mijn-moederkijken~bfa2f8a5/

13   Rob Wijnberg, *De nieuwsfabriek: hoe de media ons wereldbeeld vervormen* (Amsterdam: De Bezige Bij, 2013)

14   Leonie Breebaart, 'Daan Roovers, de nieuwe Denker des Vaderlands: "Waarom zou mijn mening interessanter zijn dan de jouwe?"', *Trouw*, 26 March 2019, www.trouw.nl/religie-filosofie/daan-roovers-de-nieuwe-denker-des-vaderlands-waarom-zoumijn-mening-interessanter-zijn-dan-de-jouwe~b68c96c45/

15   Jonathan Haidt, *The Righteous Mind: Why Good People Are Divided by Politics and Religion* (New York: Pantheon Books, 2012), p. 38

16   Ruben Mersch, *Waarom iedereen altijd gelijk heeft* (Amsterdam: De Bezige Bij, 2016)

17   Ruben Mersch, *Van mening verschillen: een handleiding* (Ghent: Borgerhoff & Lambrigts, 2018)

18   Malou van Hintum, 'Een beetje emotie kan helpen overtuigen, want met feiten alleen kom je er niet', *Trouw*, 17 March 2018, www.trouw.nl/religie-filosofie/een-beetje-emotie-kan-helpenovertuigen-want-met-feiten-alleen-kom-je-er-niet~be54f041/

19   Elke Wiss, 'Een interview met Ariane van Heijningen – inclusief schaterlach', podcast *De Denksmederij*, www.denksmederij.nl/podcast.html

20 National Research Council, *Assessing 21st Century Skills: Summary of a Workshop* (Washington DC: National Academies Press, 2011), www.nap.edu/catalog/13215/assessing-21st-century-skills-summary-of-a-workshop

21 Jan Bransen, *Gevormd of vervormd? Een pleidooi voor ander onderwijs* (Leusden: ISVW Uitgevers, 2019)

PART TWO: THE SOCRATIC ATTITUDE

1   www.collinsdictionary.com/dictionary/english/cooperation

2   Plato, *Theaetetus*, trans. Benjamin Jowett, classics.mit.edu/Plato/theatu.html

3   www.collinsdictionary.com/dictionary/english/wonder

4   *Epictetus, The Discourses and Manual*, trans. P. E. Matheson, Vol. 2 (Oxford: Clarendon Press, 1916)

5   Massimo Pigliucci, *How to Be a Stoic: Ancient Wisdom for Modern Living* (London: Ebury Press, 2017)

6   Reinoud Eleveld, 'Wu Wei, de kunst van het Niet-Doen', 23 July 2018, taotraining.nl/wu-wei-de-kunst-van-het-niet-doen/

7   Paul Bloom, 'Against Empathy', *Boston Review*, 10 September 2014, bostonreview.net/forum/paul-bloom-against-empathy

8   Reginald Rose, *Twelve Angry Men* (New York: Penguin, 2006), pp. 11–14

9   www.collinsdictionary.com/dictionary/english/elenchus

10 Plato, *The Dialogues of Plato*, Vol. 1 (1875), p. 353

11 Ibid., pp. 354–5

12 Ibid., pp. 144–5

13 Harm van der Gaag, *Wie het niet weet mag het zeggen. In de spreekkamer van de filosofische praktijk* (Leusden: ISVW Uitgevers, 2013)

PART THREE: CONDITIONS FOR QUESTIONING

1   Based on the *Enchiridion* of Epictetus, XLVI

2   Plato, *The Dialogues of Plato*, Vol. 1 (1875), p. 132

3   Ibid., p. 136

4   Ibid., p. 133

5   Hans Bolten, 'Het socratisch gesprek als instrument voor teamreflectie', *Organisatie instrumenten*, March 2003, boltentraining.nl/wp-content/uploads/2013/01/spreken-buiten-de-orde.pdf

PART FOUR: QUESTIONING SKILLS: TECHNIQUES, TIPS AND PITFALLS

1   From Wisława Szymborska, 'The Turn of the Century', trans. Joanna Trzeciak Huss, www.researchgate.net/publication/340255961_The_Turn_of_the_Century_by_Wislawa_Szymborska_trans_Joanna_Trzeciak_Huss

2   This diagram is the work of Hans Bolten and is reproduced here with his consent. Although unpublished by Bolten, he wrote down this diagram during a seminar which the author attended and it was provided by Bolten in an accompanying handout.

3   Monique Fischer, *Reflect(l)eren in het basisonderwijs* (Naarden: MF Consulting, 2017), p. 67

PART FIVE: FROM QUESTIONS TO CONVERSATION

1   www.loesje.org/ Loesje is an international free speech organisation started in Arnhem (Netherlands) in 1983. 'Loesje' is a Dutch female name, representing "a world wide collective of people who want to make the world a more positive creative place". For more information: https://en.wikipedia.org/wiki/Loesje

2   Mark Eikema, 'Praktische filosofie, het stellen van vragen en de waarde van niet-weten, met Elke Wiss', *Kramcast* (previously called *Mark in the Middle*), 17 July 2019, open.spotify.com/episode/4grLF8VQD0jiO1ranznM9c

3   Plato, *The Dialogues of Plato*, Vol. 1 (1875), p. 149

4   Ibid., pp. 149–50

5   Hans Bolten, 'Het socratisch gesprek als instrument voor teamreflectie', March 2003, boltentraining.nl/wp-content/uploads/2013/01/spreken-buiten-de-orde.pdf

6   Ariane van Heijningen, 'Ik wil confronteren', 25 November 2018, blog.denkplaats.nl/2018/11/25/ik-wil-confronteren/

Bibliography

BOOKS

Bransen, Jan, *Gevormd of vervormd? Een pleidooi voor ander onderwijs* (Leusden: ISVW Uitgevers, 2019)

Brown, Brené, *Braving the Wilderness: The Quest for True Belonging and the Courage to Stand Alone* (New York: Random House, 2017)

Epictetus, *The Discourses and Manual*, trans. P. E. Matheson, Vol. 2 (Oxford: Clarendon Press, 1916)

Fischer, Monique, *Reflect(l)eren in het basisonderwijs* (Naarden: MF Consulting, 2017)

Haidt, Jonathan, *The Righteous Mind: Why Good People Are Divided by Politics and Religion* (New York: Pantheon Books, 2012)

Kamphuis, Lammert, *Filosofie voor een weergaloos leven* (Amsterdam: De Bezige Bij, 2018)

Mersch, Ruben, *Waarom iedereen altijd gelijk heeft* (Amsterdam: De Bezige Bij, 2016)

—— *Van mening verschillen: een handleiding* (Ghent: Borgerhoff & Lamberigts, 2018)

National Research Council, *Assessing 21st Century Skills: Summary of a Workshop* (Washington DC: National Academies Press, 2011)

Pigliucci, Massimo, *How to Be a Stoic: Ancient Wisdom for Modern Living* (London: Ebury Press, 2017)

Plato, *The Dialogues of Plato*, trans. Benjamin Jowett, Vol. 1, 2nd edn (Oxford: Clarendon Press, 1875)

Rilke, Rainer Maria, *Letters to a Young Poet*, trans. M. D. Herter Norton (New York: W. W. Norton & Company, 1993), Fourth Letter

Rose, Reginald, *Twelve Angry Men* (New York: Penguin, 2006)

Rumi, *The Big Red Book: The Great Masterpiece Celebrating Mystical Love and Friendship*, trans. Coleman Barks (San Francisco: HarperOne, 2011)

van der Gaag, Harm, *Wie het niet weet mag het zeggen. In de spreekkamer van de filosofische praktijk* (Leusden: ISVW Uitgevers, 2013)

Wijnberg, Rob, *De nieuwsfabriek: hoe de media ons wereldbeeld vervormen* (Amsterdam: De Bezige Bij, 2013)

Wilde, Oscar, *The Picture of Dorian Gray* (London: Ward, Lock, 1891)

ARTICLES

Bloom, Paul, 'Against Empathy', *Boston Review*, 10 September 2014

Bolten, Hans, 'Het socratisch gesprek als instrument voor teamreflectie', *Organisatie instrumenten*, March 2003

Breebaart, Leonie, 'Daan Roovers, de nieuwe Denker des Vaderlands: "Waarom zou mijn mening interessanter zijn dan de jouwe?"', *Trouw*, 26 March 2019

de Visser, Ellen, 'Waarom je bij problemen beter geen advies kunt geven', *de Volkskrant*, 13 July 2018

Eikema, Mark, 'Praktische filosofie, het stellen van vragen en de waarde van niet-weten, met Elke Wiss', *Kramcast* (previously called *Mark in the Middle*), 17 July 2019

Eleveld, Reinoud, 'Wu Wei, de kunst van het Niet-Doen', 23 July 2018

Huigsloot, Nathalie, 'Janine Abbring: "Als je wilt weten waarom God niet bestaat, moet je naar het leven van mijn moeder kijken"', *de Volkskrant Magazine*, 6 July 2018

Lo Galbo, Carolina, 'Hoe Femke Halsema verbindend werd', *Vrij Nederland*, 25 April 2019

Neijnens, Anne, 'Jan Geurtz: De Spirituele Liefdesrelatie', *De Anne Neijnens Show*, 22 August 2018

'Socrates dood: de oerknal voor de filosofie', *Filosofie*, 10 June 2016

Tamir, Diana I. and Mitchell, Jason P., 'Disclosing Information About the Self is Intrinsically Rewarding', *Proceedings of the National Academy of Sciences* (2012), 109.21

van Heijningen, Ariane, 'Ik wil confronteren', 25 November 2018

van Hintum, Malou, 'Een beetje emotie kan helpen overtuigen, want met feiten alleen kom je er niet', *Trouw*, 17 March 2018

Ward, Adrian F., 'The Neuroscience of Everybody's Favorite Topic: Why do people spend so much time talking about themselves?', *Scientific American*, 16 July 2013

Wiss, Elke, 'Een interview met Ariane van Heijningen – inclusief schaterlach', podcast *De Denksmederij*

WEBSITES

Epictetus, *Enchiridion*, trans. Elizabeth Carter, classics.mit.edu/Epictetus/epicench.html

Plato, *Theaetetus*, trans. Benjamin Jowett, classics.mit.edu/Plato/theatu.html